ROBERT MUSIL

LITERATURE AND LIFE:
WORLD WRITERS

Selected list of titles in this series:

Complete list of titles in the series available from the
publisher on request.

ROBERT MUSIL

Lowell A. Bangerter

A Frederick Ungar Book
CONTINUUM · NEW YORK

1989

The Continuum Publishing Company
370 Lexington Avenue, New York, N.Y. 10017

Printed in the United States of America

Library of Congress Cataloging-in-Publication Data

Bangerter, Lowell A., 1941–
  Robert Musil.

  (Literature and life. World writers)
  Bibliography: p.
  Includes index.
  1. Musil, Robert, 1890–1942—Criticism and
interpretation.   I. Title.
PT2625.U8Z567   1988   833′.912   87-13695
ISBN 0-8044-2054-8

Contents

Chronology

November 6, 1880	Born in Klagenfurt, the son of Alfred and Hermine Musil.
1881–92	Spends a lonely childhood in Komotau, Steyr, and Brünn. Experiences lengthy illnesses during early school years.
1892–97	Attends military schools in Eisenstadt, Mährisch-Weißkirchen, and Vienna. Eventually breaks off his military training in favor of technical education.
1898–1901	Studies mechanical engineering at the Brünn Technical University. Passes his state examinations. Begins his earliest literary endeavors.
1901–2	Serves his mandatory year in the Austrian military.
1902–3	Works as a voluntary assistant at the Stuttgart Technical University. Begins work on *Young Törless*.
1903–8	Studies philosophy and experimental psychology at the University of Berlin and begins to contribute essays to various journals.
1906	Publishes *Young Törless*. Invents a device for use in psychological experiments with color perception.

1908	Receives his doctorate after completing a dissertation on Ernst Mach's positivism. Turns down the possibility of an assistantship position in Graz.
1908–10	Active as a writer in Berlin; contributes articles to journals while working on the two novellas of *Unions* and his first play, *The Enthusiasts*.
1910	Travels to Italy with Martha Marcovaldi.
1911–14	Works as an assistant and as a librarian at the Vienna Technical University and continues his journalistic endeavors.
April 15, 1911	Marries Martha Marcovaldi in Vienna. *Unions* appears later in the year.
1914	Works as editor of *Die Neue Rundschau* in Berlin.
1914–18	Serves as an army officer on the Italian border. Edits the *Soldaten-Zeitung* and is eventually assigned to the War-Press Office in Vienna.
1917	His father receives a patent of nobility that is hereditary.
1919–20	Works as a press archivist and consultant for the Austrian Foreign Ministry in Vienna.
1920	Spends a few months in Berlin, where he meets Ernst Rowohlt, who later becomes his publisher. Upon his return to Vienna, accepts a temporary position as consultant in the State Military Office.
1921–31	Active as a theater critic, essayist, and free-lance writer, primarily in Vienna. Works on *The Man without Qualities*.

1921	His first play, *The Enthusiasts*, appears.
1923–29	Contact with Hugo von Hofmannsthal leads to membership in the Protective League of German Writers in Austria. Occupies positions of leadership in that organization.
1923	Receives the Kleist Prize for *The Enthusiasts*. *Vinzenz and the Girl Friend of Important Men*, his second play, premieres successfully in Berlin.
1924	His parents die. The Vienna Art Prize is awarded to him. *Three Women* is published.
1927	Gives his famous speech on the occasion of Rainer Maria Rilke's death.
1929	Against his wishes, *The Enthusiasts* is performed in an embarrassingly butchered production in Berlin. Receives the Gerhart Hauptmann Prize without the expected monetary stipend.
1930	The first volume of *The Man without Qualities* is published. Despite its success, he experiences extreme financial difficulties.
1931–33	Continues his work on *The Man without Qualities* in Berlin, supported by a Musil Society that is founded by Kurt Glaser.
1933	After the first part of the second volume of *The Man without Qualities* appears, he voluntarily leaves Germany and returns to Vienna in response to the establishment of the Third Reich. Works on *The Man without Qualities* as financial problems intensify.

1934–38   A new Musil Society is formed in Vienna. It pro-
                   vides regular financial support as he struggles with
                   the pressures of writing the novel.

1935   Travels to Paris where he speaks at the Interna-
                   tional Writers' Congress for the Protection of
                   Culture.

1936   A collection of essays and short prose writings,
                   Posthumous While Still Alive, appears. Suffers a
                   stroke.

1938   Emigrates to Zurich, Switzerland by way of Italy.
                   His books are banned in Austria and Germany.

1939   Moves to Geneva. His financial situation contin-
                   ues to deteriorate.

1939–42   Works on *The Man without Qualities* under dif-
                   ficult circumstances. Receives small amounts of
                   help from various sources, especially from Pastor
                   Robert Lejeune and a small circle of friends.

April 15, 1942   Dies unexpectedly in Geneva.

1943   Martha Musil publishes the unfinished portion
                   of *The Man without Qualities*.

ROBERT MUSIL

1

A Dissatisfied Life

"I was often told in my childhood and youth: You are like your (paternal) grandfather! That meant: obstinate, energetic, also successful, hard to get along with, but said with an undertone of respect."[1] In these words from his journal, Robert Musil pinpointed early character traits that consistently affected his relationships with other people throughout his life. He described himself in another entry as a problem child whose impetuosity was the cause of substantial parental stress and worry. The difficult youngster became a lonely, misunderstood man who was often at odds with the world and seldom pleased with his own efforts. He found decision making and practical endeavor burdensome, and seemed to search in vain for security, fulfillment, and happiness.

Amid the uncertainties of the times in which he lived, Musil created complex works of literature that come to grips with his own internal and external realities, the ideas of other thinkers, possibilities and alternatives for existence, and the longings of his soul. His stories, novels, dramas, and essays examine and lay bare in minute detail the peculiarities of a world in which their author did not feel at home. In his experience and works Musil exemplified the modern literary artist as characterized by the poet and dramatist Hugo von Hofmannsthal in these words:

He lives strangely in the house of time, beneath the stairway, where all must pass by him and none regard him. . . . This dwelling unrecognized

1

in his own house, beneath the stairs, in the dark, with the dogs; foreign and yet at home . . . as a living person, thrust out by the lowest servant girl and turned away to the dogs; and without office in this house, without employment, without rights, without duty, other than to loiter and lie about and to weigh out all of this on an invisible balance, and to experience tremendous suffering, tremendous enjoyment, to possess all of this as the householder can never possess his house. . . . He . . . possesses all of this: for each of these is an open wound in his soul.[2]

At his death, Musil's spiritual wounds were still open, and his existence, like his final great novel, *The Man without Qualities*, remained curiously enigmatic and incomplete.

It was not that Musil lacked a basis or the opportunity to achieve a solid, stable position in society. The circumstances into which he was born were strongly conducive to such attainment, and his parents intended that he create a successful practical life for himself. His forebears had distinguished themselves as civil servants, military officers, scholars, and engineers. Alfred Musil, his technically gifted father, was the son of a medical doctor. Robert's maternal great-grandfather, Franz Xaver Bergauer, had played an important role in the construction and administration of the first cross-country horsecar railway from Budweis to Linz. The assumption that the young Musil would pursue a career that fit the family pattern was a significant factor in the early struggle with disparities between his own inclinations and the wishes of others for his future. Much of the tension and conflict in his life arose from his inability or unwillingness to conform to external expectations.

Continuing social isolation, spiritual and emotional deprivation on various levels, and the resulting withdrawal into his own fantasy world were the most critical formative experiences of Musil's childhood. They dominated and informed his relationships with family and peers, his attitudes toward school and other institutions, and the ultimate course of his life.

Most of Musil's recorded memories of his boyhood focus on his loneliness. The cold emptiness of his room is a constant motif in his descriptions of home. Among the things that contributed to his feelings of estrangement were recurring illnesses that took him out of school for long periods. Even when he was able to participate, he did little to involve himself constructively with the other children. He rejected invitations to join them in cultural activities, and was frequently involved in fights that won him a measure of respect while setting him apart as something of a class dictator.

Certain characteristics of his immediate environment were particularly relevant to Musil's early feelings of deprivation and isolation. Among the things that he later identified as conspicuously missing from his life were religious belief, the benefits of a normal relationship between his parents, and any sense of parental closeness, companionship, or understanding.

Alfred and Hermine Musil followed the nondevout pattern established by their own parents. Although their son was christened in accordance with the Catholic rite, he could look back and characterize the atmosphere in his family as liberal and enlightened, while viewing his home as a domain where faith did not exist and nothing was given to replace it.

Perhaps even more significant for Musil was the peculiar manner in which his parents conducted their marriage. Young Robert was especially disturbed by Hermine Musil's attitude and behavior toward his father, but he also could not understand Alfred Musil's toleration of the resulting situations. Concerning his mother, the writer later acknowledged that she appreciated his father, but that the latter did not reflect the degree of masculinity that she preferred.

The most visible consequence of this disaffection was the open presence of a second man in the inner family circle. In 1881, Hermine Musil met Heinrich Reiter, who became her intimate friend and remained close to her until she died. He was a constant guest in the Musil home, usually vacationed with the family, and even moved to Brünn to be close to Hermine. Young Robert resented Reiter, recognizing that he undermined Alfred

Musil's position and authority. That indignation, his inability to communicate effectively with his father, and the latter's failure to requite his sympathy were among the causes of a tension between Musil and his parents that was never fully resolved.

An especially interesting consequence of the young Musil's isolation was a fantasy preoccupation with his own incompleteness. He sensed that he had lost a part of himself in the infant death of a sister, Elsa, which occurred before his own birth. It has been suggested that the fascination with his missing "other half" was the primary motivation for the abduction of a little girl from a kindergarten sometime before his tenth year. It is also the seed of the complex brother-sister problem that he examined in his mature writings.[3]

By the time that Musil was ten years old, open scenes of conflict in his home had become frequent and intense. As a result, by the mutual agreement of all concerned, he was sent to the military boarding school at Eisenstadt.

According to Musil, each member of the family saw his move to Eisenstadt as the resolution of a different kind of problem. For the boy himself, it represented a victory in his struggle against allowing himself to be reared by force. He also viewed it as a step toward acceptance as a mature individual. His father, on the other hand, regarded Robert's enrollment in the academy as progress toward a life of security in harmony with family tradition. To his mother, boarding school meant the promise of the rigorous discipline that she felt her son needed as a cure for his rebellious tendencies.

Superficially, the next six years in three military academies moved Musil along the precise course that his father had envisioned for him. After overcoming an initial passionate homesickness, the youth became a successful student at Eisenstadt. In 1894, he advanced to the senior military academy at Mährisch-Weißkirchen, from which he graduated in 1897 as a second lieutenant. His subsequent enrollment in Vienna's Technical Military Academy, where he studied ballistics, permitted him to prepare for an occupation that combined the family's technical and military traditions.

In reality, the young officer left Mährisch-Weißkirchen far more undecided about his future than most of his fellow graduates. His eventual decision to reject the army in favor of a civilian engineering career was influenced by the starkly negative experiences of his years there. He saw the school as a spartan educational institution in which the cadets were treated almost like criminal prisoners. Forty years later, the horrible washing facilities, toilets, and uniforms that "defied all description" caused Musil to call the institute "the devil's anus" and led him to speculate that his obsession with cleanliness was a persisting overcompensation for the experiences of that period of his life. If not the physical details of the environment, then certainly much of the psychological debasement and spiritual agony that he suffered at the academy eventually provided substance, background, and atmosphere for his first novel, *Young Törless*.

In January 1898 shortly after he entered the Technical Military Academy, Musil abandoned the officer program and transferred to the mechanical engineering department at the technical university in Brünn. There he studied mathematics, descriptive geometry, mechanical and freehand drawing, physics, mechanics, statics, and other subjects. The results were extremely positive. In his state engineering examinations in 1899 and 1901, he received grades of "qualified" and "highly qualified" respectively. Yet despite the ease with which he concluded his technical studies, he remained uncommitted to a specific career, and the completion of his degree did not provide the anticipated basis for a stable professional future.

The years in Brünn were extremely important for what they contributed to Musil's development as a writer. During this period he encountered artistic and philosophical ideas and models that influenced and stimulated his thinking and creative work for the rest of his life. For example, he was receptive to developments in Austrian literature and art that turned away from French and

German naturalism and toward an involvement with the psychological processes and problems of man.

In later life, Musil pointed to the literary atmosphere of German modernism as an early inspiring force in his intellectual growth. He also identified several authors whose works assisted him in the process of self-perception, specifically: Ralph Waldo Emerson, Maurice Maeterlinck, Gabriele D'Annunzio, Novalis (Friedrich von Hardenberg), Jens Peter Jacobsen, Fyodor Dostoyevsky, Lev Tolstoy, and Friedrich Nietzsche. These writers influenced the manner in which the young Musil perceived the world and its realities. He was particularly impressed by Maeterlinck's modern mysticism, and he developed a special love for the figures of Raskolnikov, the doppelgänger, and the cuckold in Dostoyevsky's writings. Even more important were his reading encounters with Nietzsche. In *Beyond Good and Evil* and *The Genealogy of Morals* Musil discovered the kind of thinking that he had longed for.

Musil's exposure to the literary and philosophical currents of the time stimulated him to experiment with his own creations and ideas. In 1898, he began to record thoughts, experiences, and fragmentary literary sketches in an unstructured journal. Responding to encounters with nature, music, and love, he also wrote awkward and unrefined poems that he later described as products of a heavy, yearning heart, and writings that had little literary value.

His early prose exhibits opinions and style that are informed more by science than belles lettres. The most impressive example is found in the notes to a book that he intended to call *Blätter aus dem Nachtbuch des monsieur le vivisecteur* (Leaves from the nightbook of Monsieur Vivisector). In the notes Musil employed specific literary techniques to come to grips with his own life situation. Memories of his childhood form the basic point of departure for the projected work. In the short parts that were written, isolation is equated with happiness, and the intellectual alignment—toward the discovery of the inner self—parallels that of turn-of-the-century Austrian literature.

The brief segments from the *Nightbook* reveal the magnitude of Nietzsche's influence on the young Musil's thought. Nietzsche's equation of vivisection with the activity of the psychologist is especially important in this regard. Musil's "vivisector" is clearly related to the "vivisectors of the spirit" in *The Genealogy of Morals*, and his situation has parallels in Nietzsche's poetry.[4]

Not all of Musil's early writings are as intense as the *Nightbook*. Near the end of his stay in Brünn, he composed a series of lyrically sentimental paraphrases. The primary stimulus for these creations was a brief love affair with a local actress. A letter of 1901 indicates that he considered trying to publish the paraphrases, but a critic dissuaded him from doing so.

After passing his second engineering examination in 1901, Musil began his year of compulsory military service. From October 1, 1901, to September 30, 1902, he was a member of the Baron von Hess Infantry Regiment 49. By the end of that period he had attained the rank of sergeant. A few months later he was commissioned as a lieutenant in the reserves.

The military year represented a distinct interruption of his literary endeavors. Even his journal ceased to be a sketchbook for ideas and plans, and for the first time he began to keep a real diary.

For Musil, the months following his army duty were a peculiar time of disillusionment and frustration combined with blossoming creativity. Unable to find a professional position that suited him, he accepted an unsalaried assistantship in the materials-testing institute at the Stuttgart Technical University. There he found that technology no longer stimulated him.

Later, in looking back on the circumstances that led him to begin creating his first novel, he described the Stuttgart period as one of boredom and dissatisfaction with his profession. The city seemed foreign and unfriendly to him. He soon reached a point where he wanted to give up engineering as a career and study philosophy instead. This attitude caused him to neglect his duties and read philosophical writings during his working hours. In the afternoons, when he felt that he could no longer absorb what he had been reading, he sought diversion in writing. The result was *Young Törless*, a project that occupied his attention for more than three years.

When he left Stuttgart in 1903, Musil obtained his father's reluctant permission to enter the Friedrich Wilhelm University in Berlin, where he became a regular student of philosophy and psychology, with minors in physics and mathematics. To satisfy a technical requirement for admission to a normal course of study, he had to return to Brünn in the summer of 1904 to pass the school-leaving examination that he had previously neglected to take. From 1903 to 1908 he studied logic and the theory of knowledge, became exposed to the views of Wilhelm Dilthey and Georg Simmel, who were then teaching in Berlin, acquainted himself with gestalt and experimental psychology, explored the philosophical ideas of Ernst Cassirer, and assumed a highly critical stance with regard to the doctrines of the philosopher and psychologist Ludwig Klages. The most important professors in his major area of study were Alois Riehl and Carl Stumpf. Under the direction of Stumpf, who was never able to accept his work completely, Musil completed the dissertation that qualified him for his doctorate in February 1908.

Musil's student years also gave him contact with people who contributed substantially to his social development and, in some instances, provided character models for his literary creations. One of his very few intimate and lasting friendships began in Berlin when he became acquainted with the gifted psychologist Johannes von Allesch. (The only comparable relationship of greater duration was that of Musil and his childhood friend Gustav Donath.) For Allesch, Musil created a variation chromatometer for use in psychological experiments dealing with color perception. The device, which its inventor patented, was produced commercially and employed in experimental psychology both before and after World War I.

Musil also had meaningful encounters with several women during this period. He seemed to pursue even the most temporary of these involvements with great intensity. In a letter of 1907 to an otherwise unknown Anna, he discussed very specifically the prospect of marrying her. During the same year he was still very close to Herma Dietz, who had come to Berlin to be near him, and he was also beginning the love affair with Martha Marcovaldi that led to their marriage four years later.

Herma Dietz is a good example of a figure who found her way into Musil's writings. A simple working-class girl whom he had met in 1901 while at the Technical University in Brünn, she caused a continuing conflict between Musil and his mother. Hermine Musil felt that Herma's inferior social standing made her an unsuitable match for Robert, and she resented the girl's invited presence in Berlin. Musil's relationship with Herma Dietz later formed at least part of the basis for the novella *Tonka* in the collection *Three Women*.

Through his voluntary studies of literature during the seven years from 1903 until 1910, Musil acquired much of the intellectual, artistic, and theoretical basis for his literary career. Soon after he arrived in Berlin, he began to examine modern and classical literature from a comparative point of view in an effort to find creative orientations that suited him. In a letter he described the two specific purposes of these investigations as the search for a comparative literary method that would permit critical examination of society from a historical perspective, and the quest for a satisfactory aesthetic system. His pursuit of appropriate aesthetic models led him to the German romantics and modern mystics, while his growing vision of the need for a constructive historical literary perspective shaped his theory and practice of the novel.

The young author engaged in two kinds of writing during his university years. His first publications were essays on popular science and engineering topics. They gave him a small income to supplement resources provided by his parents. At the same time, he worked doggedly on *Young Törless*, a project that he characterized in 1903 as "this stupid novel that most certainly does not belong to me very intimately, but that I have now set my mind to complete."

The successful publication of *Young Törless* in 1906 was by no means accomplished easily. After Musil had completed the manuscript, he submitted it to three publishers, each of whom very quickly rejected it. The rapid refusals left the would-be novelist uncertain about his writing talent and caused him to turn to an acknowledged literary authority for an evaluation of his work. He selected the well-known critic Alfred Kerr, who read it and was very impressed.

Contact with Kerr was a very powerful, constructive stimulus for artistic progress. Musil later called his former mentor his greatest critical teacher. After a contract for the book's production was finally signed, Kerr agreed to assist with the correction of galley proofs, a task that remained difficult for Musil throughout his life. In addition, the critic gave his protégé suggestions concerning matters of style and form of expression. When *Young Törless* appeared, Kerr helped to promote its sale with a favorable review in a Berlin newspaper. This encouragement gave Musil needed confidence and moved him toward committing himself to a literary career.

Unfortunately, the relationship with Kerr did not remain harmonious. In 1911, Musil wrote that the connection was as good as broken off. Musil had felt insulted by the size of an honorarium for an essay that he had contributed to the periodical *Pan*, and he blamed Kerr for it. Still, in later years he regarded his association with Kerr as one of the most decisive experiences of his life.

Although the popularity of *Young Törless* established Musil's reputation as a storyteller and encouraged his artistic ambitions, it also contributed to his decision against the possibility of becoming an academic philosopher and university professor. In describing the novel's impact upon his university career, he later said that the book caused a quarrel between him and his dissertation director, Stumpf. Musil apparently became so angry with Stumpf that he then rejected an invitation to go to Graz and qualify himself as a university lecturer.

In reality, the dispute with Stumpf about *Young Törless* only added to a tension that already existed between the professor and his doctoral candidate. Musil's epistemological thesis was basically an affirmation of the physicist and philosopher Ernst Mach's positivistic teachings. Stumpf, however, was very critical of Mach and his doctrines and was initially determined to reject the dissertation. Only after repeated intense discussions about the problem did Musil succeed in obtaining Stumpf's reluctant acceptance of his paper.

After passing his doctoral examination in February 1908, Musil considered both the position in Graz and an appointment at the Munich Technical University. When the opportunity in Munich fell through, he hesitated about accepting the offer in Graz because of his involvement with Martha Marcovaldi. By that time, their relationship was already very strong, and neither of them really wanted to go to Graz. In that context, Stumpf's attack against *Young Törless* precipitated the decision to remain in Berlin because it challenged Musil's perception of himself as a budding author. A later diary entry admits that the couple's reluctance to go to Graz could have been overcome, were it not for the fact that Musil already had "naïve hopes" about the future of his writing career.

These "naïve hopes" were not based only on the success of *Young Törless*. Soon after Musil's graduation, Franz Blei, the editor of *Hyperion*, asked him to write a story for the publication. Musil responded with "Das verzauberte Haus", (The enchanted house), an early version of *The Temptation of Quiet Veronica*. Impressed with the quality of the narrative and its timely completion, Blei immediately requested a second contribution. Musil accepted the assignment, assuming that it could be completed as easily as the earlier one. When the new creation refused to come forth, he described his frustration as being like that of a cat waiting in vain in front of a mouse hole. Neither the commissioned story nor the drama that he began writing at about the same time was completed before he left Berlin.

The struggle with his artistic creations caused Musil to consider contributing essays and articles to newspapers and periodicals in order to support himself financially, but he could not bring himself to do it on a continuing basis. He regarded writing for the feuilletons, even the major respected ones, as being something repulsive. When his parents finally refused to provide more money, he tried to obtain a position as literary critic for the *Berliner Zeitung*. The attempt failed, and he had no alternative but to accept a librarianship that his father obtained for him at the Vienna Technical University.

The most significant development in Musil's life during the next few years was his marriage to Martha Marcovaldi, a Jewish painter who was seven years his senior. When he left Berlin in September 1910 he and Martha spent three months in Italy before he began his library work. By then, they would already have been man and wife were it not for the difficulties that she had in obtaining a divorce. (Her young husband's unexpected death had ended her first marriage after only two years. She had then studied art in Berlin, and had married an Italian merchant with whom she had two children. When that relationship soured, she returned to Berlin to live with her sister, but Enrico Marcovaldi initially refused to let her terminate their marriage.)

As it was, the preparations for the wedding were extremely complicated. Because divorce was a problem in Austria, it was first necessary for Martha to be adopted by a Hungarian in order to obtain a foreign citizenship. She could then obtain a divorce in a Hungarian court. In order to avoid conflict with the Catholic church, both she and Musil converted to Protestantism prior to the wedding that finally took place on April 15, 1911.

Martha proved to be the ideal companion for Musil. Their

relationship was consistently so intense that he came to view her as another side of himself. In his diary he described her as something that he had become and that had become him. The impact that she eventually had upon every aspect of his existence was enormous. Specific experiences with her provided substantial substance for his mature writings, while her constant devotion and unfailing belief in him were a sustaining force that enabled him to continue his work during the most trying times. It is certainly no exaggeration, when Karl Dinklage, Musil's biographer, insists: "One thing remains certain in any case. Martha was for Robert Musil the intellectual, spiritual, physical complement that was necessary for him to become what he is today for us and the world."[5]

The immediate happiness of his marriage made up in part for the lack of fulfillment that Musil found in his artistic and professional activities during the prewar years in Vienna. His struggles with his writing were especially frustrating. It was not that he continued to suffer from an inability to generate viable ideas, as he had done for a time in Berlin. On the contrary, he wrote and rewrote portions of *Unions* and various sections of *The Man without Qualities*, composing many variations of the stories and their parts. The real problem was that he had extreme difficulty in arriving at versions that finally satisfied him.

His painstaking efforts to perfect *Unions* produced a book in 1911 that failed to attain the popular success of *Young Törless*. The reading public found the stories very difficult to understand and never warmed to them. By 1914, Musil had not overcome the disappointment of this particular failure. The bitterness and resignation that he still felt are apparent in words written to the poet Rainer Maria Rilke concerning the two novellas: "You will not like them, I fear. But since they also only represent an episode for me, you will not hold that against me."

Musil's library position at the technical university was somewhat kinder to him in terms of material reward. During the course of staffing changes caused by the head librarian's death in 1911,

Musil was promoted to librarian second class and given a corresponding increase in pay. By 1913, however, his dissatisfaction with the position had become so intense that he was desperately looking for other employment alternatives. Pleading illness, he requested leaves of absence and spent his time writing. Finally, at the end of 1913, he returned to Berlin, where he remained until the outbreak of the war. From there he requested that he be released from his responsibilities at the library so that he could accept a more desirable position as editor of *Die Neue Rundschau*.

While still in Vienna, Musil had begun to write for several periodicals, including *Die Neue Rundschau*, Franz Blei's *Der Lose Vogel*, and the expressionistic journals *Die Aktion* and *Die Weißen Blätter*. He contributed articles on politics, character sketches, and items of literary criticism. The editorship with *Die Neue Rundschau* enabled him to intensify those endeavors. Like his creative writings, however, the works on public affairs did not satisfy him. He later declared that although they were perhaps not uninteresting, he did not consider any of them to be substantial. His readers, however, found his essays clever, full of ideas, and well-thought-out. The literary reviews that appeared in *Die Neue Rundschau* are particularly powerful and contain analysis and commentary of the highest quality.

Musil's prewar political essays reflect a turning point in his sociopolitical consciousness. He had spent his home years in an atmosphere that was dominated by distaste for politics and a complete lack of understanding regarding political issues. In the articles that he wrote in 1913 there evolved a basic position that he later regarded as the "primary illusion" of his life, specifically, that "the spirit, without prejudice to everything that occurred on a practical level, was elevating itself step by step, . . . that the time of its catastrophes was past."

At the outbreak of World War I, Musil was called into the army and sent to southern Tirol, where he remained for three years. He was initially charged with organizational responsibilities pertaining to border security and the development, maintenance, and strengthening of frontline positions. Health problems confined him to military hospitals in the spring of 1916, after which he edited the army newspaper *Soldaten-Zeitung*. Under his direction, the publication emphasized imperial unity and campaigned against Italian irredentism. During the war, he received decorations and promotions for his committed service, but he often felt that they were empty compensation for the sacrifices that he made.

By 1918 Musil had attained the rank of captain. He was then ordered to the War Press Office in Vienna, where he led a special propaganda group that published the weekly patriotic newspaper *Heimat* until after the end of the war.

With the exception of his military newspaper activities, the war years were a relatively sterile time for Musil. His human surroundings did little to encourage him to write. As he later recalled his wartime experience, there was an overwhelming sense of having been surrounded by people who never read anything except the newspaper, and who regarded writing books, other than technical ones, as something indecent. Nevertheless, in that environment he did have time to observe, ponder, and collect material that became valuable for his postwar writings. His impressions of the southern Tirolean countryside, for example, are integrated into the landscape descriptions in the novellas *Grigia* and *The Lady from Portugal*.

After the war, Musil was faced with the renewed question of how to make a living. In 1919, Martha Musil wrote to her daughter that it was difficult for them to decide whether to live in Berlin or Vienna.[6] Her husband would have preferred Berlin. In anticipation of beginning to work again as a publicist, he had already resumed writing essays, and he and Martha had taken only temporary lodgings in a convalescent home owned by the philanthropist Dr. Eugenie Schwarzwald in the small town of Mödling. Unfortunately, the inquiries about positions in Berlin remained fruitless, and he was forced to stay in Vienna as a press-clipping archivist for the Foreign Office.

While visiting Berlin in the summer of 1920, he attempted to obtain the position with *Die Neue Rundschau* that he had held before the war. Although Samuel Fischer, the owner of the periodical, was willing to hire him, he could not meet Musil's salary demands, and the unhappy writer returned to Vienna in disappointment.

For the next two years, Musil was an educational advisor in the Bureau of Military Affairs, where he gave lectures on pedagogy, career orientation, and psychotechnology. The work did not appeal to him, and he refused to accept a continuing appointment that would have given him financial security. That decision was particularly significant in light of his penchant for order in his external affairs and his insistence upon good food and the best clothing as minimal requirements for an acceptable standard of living. His rejection of the permanent position cost him his job in 1922, when austerity measures were introduced. Because he was entitled to six months notice before termination, he continued to receive a government salary into 1923, but after that, for the remainder of his life he lived only from his literary earnings and the private help of friends and admirers.

In his diary, Musil described the war's initial impact on his creativity. It was as though a disease or its accompanying fever had come over him. His return to active literary endeavor in Vienna was necessary to the restoration of his spiritual and even physical health. The tedium of his civil service seemed to rob him of his strength. In the summer of 1919 Martha complained that her husband was worn out, suffering from chronic headaches, and very much in need of rest.[7] Under the circumstances, his writing on *The Man without Qualities* and his first play, *Die Schwärmer* (The enthusiasts), became a refuge in which he could close himself off somewhat from what took place in the world.

Late in 1919, *The Enthusiasts* occupied his attention to the point that he was compelled to write to a friend, saying that he was so deeply involved in it, that he could do nothing else until it was finished. He expected to accomplish it by the end of the year, but as was typical for his work, completion of the project required more time than he had anticipated. When the play was finally ready, he had great difficulty in finding a publisher for it. Eventually, his friend Franz Blei mediated an agreement with Sibyllen-Verlag in Dresden, and the work appeared in 1921.

The reviews of the book were primarily positive and even enthusiastic. Critics pointed to new perspectives that *The Enthusiasts* opened for the theater, and Musil began to hope that the piece would be staged by one of the prominent directors of the time. The drama received additional recognition in the form of the Kleist Prize for 1923. While making the award, the novelist Alfred Döblin praised Musil's "free and definite masculine spirit" and his "grand view of the social tensions of our time."[8]

Despite the book's success, *The Enthusiasts* did not launch Musil into a happy career as a stage dramatist. His attempts to have the play produced brought nothing but frustration and disappointment. One director after another rejected it because of its length and theatrical unsuitability. Musil finally accepted the fact that the contemporary theater would not do justice to his material, and when the play finally opened in a small Berlin theater in 1929, it did so against his wishes. As he had feared, the production was a dismal failure. The director had slashed the text mercilessly, leaving only the shell of the original creation. Musil was devastated by the butchery of his work, and its misfortune contributed to a growing bitterness that he never overcame.

The literary acclaim given *The Enthusiasts* after its publication was only part of the positive response to Musil's writing efforts during the early 1920s. For a short period of time he actually enjoyed a moderate degree of prosperity as a result of a very fruitful and many-sided productivity. The other endeavors that began to establish him on a sound footing, both financially and artistically, were his essayistic ventures, a second play, and *Three Women*.

Musil continued to contribute to various periodicals only out of necessity. Even though he had still not warmed to the idea, he agreed to write for *Die Neue Rundschau*, in order to work off his debts to the publisher Samuel Fischer. Early in the decade he wrote nearly sixty informative and engaging articles about theater performances, exhibits, and literary publications. Almost two-thirds of them appeared in *Die Prager Presse* in 1921 and 1922. Additional essays were placed in *Bohemia, Die Neue Rundschau, Der Neue Merkur, Die Literarische Welt, Die Deutsche Allgemeine Zeitung*, and other newspapers and journals. In November 1921 the income from these writings enabled him to purchase an apartment in Vienna's third district. It remained his home for the rest of his years in Austria. By 1923, the success of other writings had encouraged him to give less attention to criticism as a vocation, and thereafter he wrote only occasional essays.

The literary creations that finally established Musil's broader public reputation were the play Vinzenz and the Girl Friend of Important men (*Vinzenz und die Freundin bedeutender Männer*) and the stories of *Three Women*. Ironically, both books are fruits of a time when the author saw himself as living a dissatisfied and uneasy life because the things he was doing were not what he felt he should do. Although the drama was written "only in fun" and the third novella of the collection was described during the writing process as "very bad and confused" and "awful," *Vinzenz and the Girl Friend of Important Men* and *Three Women* are the achievements that coincide with their creator's reception of the Vienna Literature Prize for 1924, and his accompanying rise to prominence.

Vinzenz and the Girl Friend of Important Men accomplished for Musil what *The Enthusiasts* could not. It gave him positive exposure on the stage. When the satirical piece opened at Berlin's Lustspielhaus in 1923, Berthold Viertel's production was an immediate success. Musil himself received vigorous applause and took repeated bows. Subsequent performances during the next year in Teplitz, Prague, and Vienna featured extraordinary ac-

complishment by Lore Busch in the leading female role, and
they were given high praise in the press.

While Musil was enjoying the public acclaim that *Vinzenz
and the Girl Friend of Important Men* brought him, *Three Women*
was published in Berlin. The volume brought together *Grigia*
and *The Lady from Portugal*, two stories that had appeared in-
dependently in 1923, and *Tonka*, a problematic, partially autobiographical novella of peculiar intensity. These three narratives
formed an important step in Musil's presentation of his grapplings
with the deepest problems of his own inner life. They have come
to be regarded by many critics as the most artistically successful
of his works.

With increased visibility came new participation in the cultural establishment of the time. Prior to 1923 Musil had avoided
any substantial association with major contemporary literary figures. At the end of the war, he had joined Kasimir Edschmid
and others in signing the program declaration of the Political
Council of Intellectual Workers, but that had been his only real
cooperative involvement with other authors. In 1923, however,
Hugo von Hofmannsthal introduced him into the Protective
League of German Writers in Austria. He was quickly elected to
that organization's directorate as Hofmannsthal's deputy, and he
continued to serve there in a leadership capacity until 1929.

The fame and relative prosperity of the early 1920s may well
have had negative consequences for Musil in the long run. They
seem to have given him a false sense of lasting security that made
it difficult for him to cope with the less-favorable fiscal realities
of the second half of the decade. He believed that his new stature
placed him in a position of strength from which he could claim
financial support that would enable him to give undivided attention to his monumental masterpiece *The Man without Qualities*.
Moreover, he assumed that he could do so regardless of the
amount of time that the undertaking might require. Accordingly,
he greatly reduced his essayistic endeavors and turned away from

any serious effort to complete the many shorter projects that he had considered during the postwar years. As a result, his continuing work on the novel was accompanied by a loss in popularity with the public, conflict with his publisher, friends, and others, and increasingly bleak financial circumstances. These last were compounded by misfortunes for which he was not even responsible. In 1929, for example, he received the Gerhart Hauptmann Prize only to see that honor transformed into a hollow mockery when there was no money available to pay him the customary stipend.

Although he found it difficult to promote his work publicly, Musil did begin to make a few overt attempts to regain his audience's attention. In 1926, an interview with Oskar Maurus Fontana, a noted critic, spotlighted *The Man without Qualities*. Increasingly disturbed by a lack of favorable exposure in the media, he used his famous Rilke speech of 1927 to chastize the press for its inability to appreciate the writer. While these presentations of his concerns were valuable for what they communicated about Musil and his work, they did little to improve his immediate personal situation, and his problems continued to intensify.

A primary cause of Musil's ever-unhappier plight was his consistent dissatisfaction with the portions of the novel that he completed. Incessant revision and rewriting caused production to drag on interminably, and Ernst Rowohlt grew reluctant to pay the advances that the author requested. The only thing that kept the publisher from terminating support was his recognition of Musil's desperation. He later explained that he had continued to back the project because Musil had threatened to shoot himself if he could not finish the novel. Although others had said similar things to him, Musil was the only one he believed. It was for that reason that he published Musil's work.[9]

The pressure to produce had an adverse effect on Musil's mental health. In his relationships to his surroundings, an obsessively defensive stance manifested itself openly in his behavior. In his workroom and the cafés that he passionately visited, he insisted on seating arrangements that placed him with a protective wall at his back where he could watch both windows and doors for approaching "attackers." More serious were depressions and other psychological disturbances that repeatedly prevented him from working. In order to deal with these problems, he began psychoanalytic therapy in 1928, under the care of Dr. Hugo Lukácz, a disciple of Alfred Adler. Although the treatments were eventually successful, they did not prevent the nervous breakdown that Musil suffered in 1929. The lingering effects of it caused him to compare the work of writing his novel to that of running a sausage grinder that he could not drive any faster. During this period he was constantly irritated by trivial disturbances, and increasing friction developed between him and Rowohlt. As a result, he struggled with depression and found himself unable to maintain a creative and productive frame of mind.

Musil's spiritual debility was compounded by his dire fiscal circumstances. On January 6, 1930, he entered in his diary: "We only have enough to live on for a few weeks. Martha wants me to make that clear to myself." Subsequent entries underscore the seriousness of the couple's financial plight before the publication of the first volume of *The Man without Qualities* in 1931. With only brief periods of respite, the writer and his wife lived on the brink of abject poverty for most of their remaining years together. No matter what they or their would-be benefactors did to alleviate the constant worry about resources, there was seldom more than enough money to meet immediate needs, and the future seemed to hold more threat than promise.

Musil had hoped that completion of the first part of *The Man without Qualities* would appease Rowohlt enough to win continued monetary support and a certain amount of breathing room for his work on the remainder of the novel. Unfortunately, the publisher did not cooperate. In a letter to his friend Johannes von Allesch, the author expressed his growing frustration, complaining bitterly about Rowohlt's refusal to advance more than a minimal amount of money toward the completion of the second part of the novel. He accused Rowohlt of hiding behind commercial considerations, and he was afraid that the publisher intended to abandon the project if it were not financially successful. From Musil's point of view, the resulting pressures made his working conditions intolerable.

In September 1931 Rowohlt tried to force Musil to work faster. He limited his monetary commitment to an additional six months' support. Under that kind of threat, Musil decided that he could not complete the novel in Vienna and moved to Berlin to a more favorable climate for his work.

The publisher's attempt to use financial leverage to speed the creative process was only partly successful. Contributions from a private Musil Society founded by Professor Kurt Glaser took some of the sting out of Rowohlt's curtailment of payments and enabled Musil to take more time with his writing. Nevertheless, the organization's resources were not sufficient to buy him sufficient time to complete the novel, and he finally had to prepare a portion of the material for publication. The first thirty-eight chapters of book 2 appeared in March 1933. Shortly after the volume reached the bookstores, Musil was named that year's recipient of the Goethe Prize.

Although he was under no direct compulsion, Musil left Berlin for Vienna when the Nazis came into power. Despite his apolitical stance regarding contemporary events and his unwillingness to become actively involved in opposition to the new regime, he could not support the emerging system's "naked ugliness." Years later, when his books had been banned in Germany and Austria in the aftermath of the Anschluss, and his financial condition had become more precarious than ever, he remained firm in his decision to have nothing to do with the Nazi dictatorship. The Hamburg publisher Eugen Claasen, acting for the German Propaganda Ministry, offered to mediate his restoration to acceptance within the Reich, insisting that the banning of Musil's writings was a misunderstanding. Musil rejected the functionary's guarantee of security to avoid the political commitment that was expected in return. After that, when the war broke out, he adopted an attitude of resignation toward the terrible events that were reported. "It is the Deluge," he said in explanation of his behavior. "We are powerless against the Deluge."

The only thing that kept Musil's "ark" from sinking during those last turbulent years in Vienna was the organization of a second Musil Society that contributed modest monthly sums for his maintenance from 1934 to 1938. Dr. Bruno Fürst, who was instrumental in bringing the small group of supporters together, made the impoverished writer the object of a personal crusade. He persuaded people who had never heard of Musil to donate money regularly, placed his country house at the author's disposal for vacations, and mediated an agreement in which Rowohlt sold the publishing rights to *The Man without Qualities* to Bermann-Fischer Verlag that had just opened a branch in Vienna.

Motivated by these signs of interest in his work, Musil began to show some renewed confidence in his ability to contribute to European cultural life. Although the primary emphasis of his effort remained *The Man without Qualities*, his notebooks of the period reveal rekindled interest in projects that had been dormant. Among them were a collection of essays, a utopian novel, and his autobiography.

Gradually, he also began to make himself more accessible to the public. In 1935, he accepted an invitation to travel to Paris and address the International Writers' Congress for the Defense of Culture. Later that same year, he read from his works in Switzerland. His increasing visibility was undoubtedly a factor in a request from Humanitas Verlag in Zurich that he collect for publication his short prose sketches that had appeared in scattered newspapers and periodicals during the previous two decades, a project that came to fruition in 1936 in the volume *Posthumous While Still Alive*.

It is indicative of the tension that existed between Musil and the external world that none of these experiences brought him any real degree of fulfillment. His assessment of his role in the

Paris meeting revealed his unhappiness with what took place. He specifically decried the political tone of the conference, because he felt that it had placed him in the awkward position of having disappointed his hosts. He had accepted the invitation without being aware of what was really expected of him. As a result, he had had to improvise with respect to his lecture, a fact that left him completely dissatisfied with his own performance. Similarly, the other ventures left him frustrated. The reading in Switzerland displeased him because the honorarium was too small, and *Posthumous While Still Alive* remained a work that he had "actually published unwillingly."

The volume of short prose with its ironically suggestive title was Musil's last completed book. Within the context of other events that conveyed the same message, it was like an omen that signaled the end of his career. Beginning in 1936, each of his major efforts to maintain and justify his existence ended in some failure that openly defied his right to continue living and writing.

On one level, his personal habits accelerated the deterioration of his health. For years he had employed smoking as a means to cope with his problems. According to his diary, he rationalized his smoking by subscribing to the view that life was something unpleasant that could be overcome by smoking. When he subjected his weakened body to the rigorous, prolonged exercise that he believed would maintain his physical well-being, the result was a stroke that left his health permanently unstable.

In the practical realm, endeavors to improve Musil's financial situation led only to frustration. His request for a government pension based on his civil service after World War I was turned down in 1937. He reluctantly prepared an additional twenty chapters of *The Man without Qualities* for publication by Bermann-Fischer, somehow sensing even then that the effort was in vain. "I am unhappily engaged here in finishing a new portion of my novel for late autumn," he wrote, "for it will hardly be possible for me to achieve a segment that will be worth publishing." When Hitler's troops marched into Austria, Musil was in the process of correcting the galleys. The Nazi seizure of the publishing house immediately halted that phase of the novel's production.

The exile years in Switzerland—first in Zurich, then in Geneva—were a period of never-ending humiliation. Musil was shattered by the necessity to beg for help from relief organizations, prominent writers and others with connections to foreign countries, friends, admirers, acquaintances, religious groups, and anyone else who would listen. The letters that he wrote between his departure from Vienna in 1938 and his death in 1942 are filled with pleas for assistance, complaints about what he saw as the indifference of those in a position to render aid, and expressions of thanks for small contributions, each of which seemed to come at just the last moment before disaster.

His only escapes from the constant misery and insecurity were a few special friendships and a strong commitment to work on *The Man without Qualities*. Pastor Robert Lejeune, who provided monetary support and help with various immediate problems, offered Musil a focus of warmth that tempered the pain of estrangement and gave encouragement and solace. The novel gave its author a portion of himself to cling to in his uncertainty. But even Lejeune and his work often failed to give him the succor that he needed. A few terse lines from his diary, written near the end of 1939, convey the magnitude of the ongoing despair that constantly threatened to overwhelm him: "Often the strong need to break off everything. Then consider my life to be a failure. Have no faith in myself, but working, carry myself onward, and every two or three days what I am writing seems to be momentarily important." As his life approached its end, it was only that fleeting sense of the significance of *The Man without Qualities* that sustained him at all.

On April 15, 1942, after spending the morning working on the novel, Musil suffered a cerebral hemorrhage while preparing to bathe before the midday meal. In describing to her daughter the material that he had been working on just before his death,

Martha Musil stated that he had written the last incomplete chapter in twenty versions. According to her account, he went upstairs after completing a final beautiful sentence, with which he was apparently satisfied.[10] Her assessment of the closing moments of her husband's life suggests that it ended on a brief note of fulfillment, in quiet contrast to the dissatisfaction with which he typically responded to his experiences.

2

The Other Condition:
Young Törless

"He was aware that everything he did was merely a game, merely something to help him over this time at school, this larval period of his existence. It was without relation to his real personality, which would emerge only later, at some time still a long way off in the future." In this passage from *Young Törless*, Musil describes the mental attitudes of a protagonist who lives in a transitional world between the emptiness of childhood and the complete fulfillment of self-discovery. The cadet Törless observes, analyzes, and experiments with that larval environment, struggles with the changes that are occurring within himself, and seeks for clues to his own identity in his encounters with other figures.

The quest has two parts. First, Törless must find a viable doorway through which he can pass into the "Other Condition," a world that lies beyond the boundaries of his current limited existence and is the proper home of the person that he may become. Only in the process of exploring the alternate realm can he then find the path into the depths of his own soul, where he can penetrate the façades and peel away the masks that now conceal all but the faint and shadowy outlines of his hidden self.

These problems of personal growth and the struggle toward self-definition are the focus not only of Musil's first novel, but also of his oeuvre as a whole. Through a process of investigation and illumination of different alternatives for thought and action,

the author typically illustrates the means by which the individual
may encounter life governed by new parameters and thereby come
closer to understanding and realizing his own potential. *Young
Törless*, with its treatment of the protagonist's progress through
the difficult period of puberty, sets the pattern for the later, more
mature works. These present from various perspectives the task
of examining and responding to the many possibilities that exist
at critical turning points in life.

The plot of *Young Törless* is not especially complex. It is
framed in the central figure's experiences at a military boarding
school somewhere in a remote part of the Austrian Empire. After
an initial period of adjustment, during which Törless fails in an
attempt to establish a friendship with a young prince, he begins
an association with two dictatorial classmates, Reiting and
Beineberg. The three cadets share various adventures, including
visits to a local prostitute and other escapes from the monotony
of the school routine. When they discover that a fourth student,
Basini, has been stealing money from lockers, they use the pretext
of punishing him for his crimes to force him into a kind of slavery.
Each of the conspirators carries out a personal experiment with
the victim, subjecting him to humiliation, brutality, and overt
sexual demands. Eventually, the affair is exposed, Basini is suspended from school and Törless is dismissed on grounds of emotional instability. The other two participants seem to emerge un-
scathed. They are permitted to remain at the academy and
complete their education.

There has been some tendency in Musil scholarship to regard
Young Törless as a creation that deals with the challenges and
crises of puberty from the perspective of emerging trends in psy-
choanalysis. Harry Goldgar, for example, suggests that the book
is "the earliest novel of any sort in any language to show specific
Freudian influence."[1] While it is certainly possible to relate the
central character's development and his experiences with other
figures to a general Freudian behavior scheme, there is no specific
evidence in the text or in Musil's diaries and letters that the author

was directly affected by Freud's ideas. More important, Musil's comments about his work disclaim the presence of psychology for its own sake in *Young Törless*. In discussing the book's relationship to the psychological novel, he insisted that his creation contained no real psychology, or that what there was had been handled arbitrarily and amateurishly. At most he acknowledged the presence of a few psychological elements that he had combined as he saw fit.

In this connection, it is important to understand that Musil viewed psychology in literature as only a vehicle for conveying substance, not a purpose for art.[2] Accordingly, in identifying his literary approach in *Young Törless*, he disassociated it from any kind of naturalism and labeled it a symbolic work, illustrative of an idea. This posture pinpointed what would later become a defining characteristic of his art: the illustration of ideas.

The primary notion around which Musil built his story is the perception of the adolescent as a basically featureless potential being, a larva. It was not, however, simply the portrayal of such an individual that interested him, but rather the presentation and indication of "what is unfinished in this unfinished person."[3] In the narrative process, the author outlines his subject's reactions to the growing awareness of his own incompleteness, and his attempts to achieve the transition from his current state to an as yet unknown identity. The young cadet's struggle then leads him to explore and experiment with various confusing possibilities for breaking through to a higher plane of existence.

From the outset of his stay at the boarding school, a tension exists between Törless and the realm that he has entered. Initially, he has difficulty in adjusting to the feeling of being cut off from his family and the past. His first reaction is to reject the new surroundings and try to escape back into the world from which he has come. The narrator describes him as living only in the steady stream of letters that he writes home. For the insecure cadet, events and experiences in the external world become shadowy and meaningless, having no greater impact upon him than markers of time's passage. His homesickness finally abates, but it is replaced only by an emptiness within him, rather than acceptance of his situation. It is from the perspective of that internal void that he begins to observe the "cocoon" around him, searching for new substance for his life.

Two characteristics of Törless's environment have profound impact upon his efforts to cope with what he encounters at the institute. The first is temporal and physical isolation. During the time that he spends at the school, the youth continues to struggle mentally with the problems of his break with the past and the barrier that exists between himself and the future. While visiting the prostitute Božena with Beineberg, Törless hears the woman mock his companion's claim that his mother no longer exists for him. The boy's response to Božena's words is described as a recollection of his earlier ideas about himself coupled with the realization that he is leaving his former world behind him and betraying the image of his mother and father.

The boy's efforts to free himself from the past and progress to the future always seem to end just short of reaching the intended goal. At a typical point in the narrative he appears to be on the verge of something that remains ahead of him, just beyond his grasp. Although he sees himself as prepared to dispose of the burdens and hindrances that bind him to the past, and to focus his complete attention on the steps that he must now take into the future, he never makes the transition. It is always "tomorrow" that a concentrated mental analysis will be carried out, giving him the clarity of insight that he needs.

Physical isolation is a factor that shapes the experience and development of all of the academy's cadets. The school is presented as a place where youthful energies are confined behind dismal walls. Because they have no other outlet, these energies stimulate ribald fantasies in the cadets' imaginations, fantasies that lead many of them astray. Within Törless, the solitude fosters a strong feeling of loneliness that becomes a focus of justification for his personal behavior. He rationalizes base actions as belonging by nature to the state in which he exists. That which is shameful is simply "one solitude more," against which he is helpless, and he finds himself unable to fight the temptations that arise out of a growing sensitivity to sensual things. The problem has its most intense manifestation in his homosexual relationship with Basini, an encounter that challenges Törless's very concept of his own identity.

The description of his internal response to what is happening to him emphasizes the breakdown of his resistance as a product of his aloneness. As he considers the lust that has slowly taken hold of him while seeming to come at him from every trivial experience, he finds it to be almost overwhelming. Its impact upon him is twofold. On the one hand, it moves him in the direction of resignation. On the other, it promotes within him the rationalization that his own solitude gives him all the justification that he needs for anything that he wants to do.

Personal isolation is the most consistent feature of Törless's life. Siegfried Rönisch stresses the fact that even though the young man eventually resolves the inward confusion that is stimulated by his boarding-school experiences, at the end of the novel he remains as isolated and lonely as he was at the beginning.[4]

The second critical aspect of Törless's surroundings is the human population of the larval world, especially the students with whom he interacts. As he tries to adapt to his situation, Törless imitates the behavior of his rough companions, Reiting and Beineberg, even though he is indifferent to the things that motivate their actions. His reason for doing so is a combination of his own sense of aloneness and the lure of their apparent participation in a defined social structure. An important part of what he learns from watching them is what it means to be a political leader. In effect, he and his classmates operate within a small autonomous state of sorts, and the dominant role that the two bullies play in that self-contained system instills within Törless a degree of respect for them.

Interpreters of the novel are quick to decode the microcosmic world of the academy as a symbol for the external society. There are clear parallels between the roles played by the institution's staff and the contemporary political establishment, and between the students and the stratified citizenry. Concerning the latter relationship, Uwe Baur has observed that the visible dualities in the personalities of specific cadets "reflect the split nature of the middle-class individual."[5] In that respect, the novel is another variation on the theme of Faustian man.

More important than the characters' reflection of the social problems of their time, is their prefiguration of the human community's future. Like Törless, the other students are "larvae" in a transitional state from which they will emerge to claim their true identities. The seeds of the social and political patterns that they will create are contained in their interactions with one another in the enclosed sphere of the school.

Viewed from that perspective, Musil's portrayals of the cadets, collectively and individually, including their evolving attitudes and calculated actions, are very revealing. Adjectives such as "animalistic" and "bestial" are used commonly to describe everything from general sleeping habits to social interchange. On a more selective personal level, Beineberg's very appearance is termed "obscene." Especially significant is the absence of the moral power to resist temptation in the primary figures of the novel, with the result that they are completely indifferent to the things that seek to constrain them only on the basis of their moral correctness. The ultimate product of this pool of negative traits and tendencies is a total insensitivity to basic human worth and dignity. That disregard for the value of life is best illustrated in Beineberg's justification of his notion that it does not matter if they torment Basini to death just for fun. He insists that a creature like Basini can have no possible meaning for the processes of the universe as a whole.

In 1903, while he was still working on *Young Törless*, Musil wrote to a friend that he had been seeking a literary method that would "make it possible for us to observe ourselves a little bit historically." With his creation of the institute and its population, he produced a concrete example of the kind of writing that such an approach might generate. Only much later in life did he realize that his first novel had depicted with peculiar certainty at least a portion of the Nazi system's human origins. In a diary entry of the late 1930s, he placed *Young Törless* in its true historical perspective when he identified the brutally tyrannical students Reiting and Beineberg as "today's dictators *in nucleo.*"

Initially, Törless assumes that contemplation and analysis of his surroundings will enable him to define and establish himself. He watches the interactions of others and expects to find in them the answers to questions concerning his own purpose and direction in life. Even his involvement in various activities has a strangely vicarious quality to it, such that he appears to withdraw mentally and observe himself going through the motions of participation.

The results of his observations remain inconclusive. He is conscious of the need to understand the things that confront him, but what he sees tells him very little, primarily because he has difficulty in distinguishing between façade and truth. The narrator describes him as going astray because he mistakes for reality the shadows that he sees. Even when he begins to discern the presence of the masks, he remains unable to penetrate to what lies beneath them. The natural explanation for things seems only to remove a thin outer layer from the packaging of the secret without actually exposing the elusive truth that appears to glimmer behind the unimportant trappings. Accordingly, his inability to identify specifically with the other students and the animalistic aspect of their lives contributes to the elusiveness of a concrete self-image. His being takes on an indefinite quality of helplessness that bars the way to self-understanding. As a consequence, the point of reference where he must begin a more active search for personal identity is a state in which it appears that he has "no character at all."

The transition from passive consideration of his situation to active involvement in the process of self-definition is very difficult for Törless. He accepts the idea that tangible experience holds the key to the information that he wants, and he suspects what form it must take, but he does not know how to generate that experience. He therefore waits for something to happen, and his vision of what must come is colored by the changes that occur within himself, and by what he has observed in the people around him.

At one point, for example, he associates his condition with earlier experiences in which he visited museums and saw paintings that he did not understand. Then, he had stood in front of the pictures, waiting for something that never happened, something that he could not identify. Now, he has a similar experience. As he tries to envision what it is that he is waiting for, he concludes that it must be something astonishing and monstrous, and, more important, something bestially sensual that he connects in peculiar fashion with images of women's soiled petticoats, roughened hands, and squalid dwellings, and with the very filth of the court-yards that seems to cling to and stain him.

While he waits for the grand illuminating event that will unlock the door to his own identity, Törless gives brief consideration to the sources from which others obtain personal enlightenment. He listens to Beineberg tell about his officer father who read only works of Indian philosophy that took on the character of direct revelations and keys to a different kind of life, much as had the writings of medieval alchemists and magicians. But such things make no impression on Törless because they provide no real means for penetration of the self. Even later, when he actively examines the teachings of Immanuel Kant, philosophy fails to offer him a viable basis for progress toward his goal. Concerning the results of Törless's encounter with Kant, Frederick G. Peters has written:

Törless's Kant experience serves first to reconfirm the opposition between himself and the adult world of reason, and second to extend this opposition into the realm of learning and philosophy, which he also now rejects as being superficial and uninteresting. As Törless comes to regard the world of passions as the only reality, the everyday world of teachers, parents, and school seems to become by comparison even more stupid, boring, and trivial.[6]

The growing alienation of the young cadet from the realm of mundane experience is accelerated by the continued failure of known entities to provide access to the things that he does not understand. When he seeks answers to his questions in memories of his parents and their relationship to each other, he wonders what they felt. Love comes to his mind as a concept, but he concludes that it was not present because love can only be experienced by the young and lonely who can sit at open windows and feel abandoned and misunderstood, while they are unable to explain their feelings and yearnings. Again he fails to find the needed clues to the future, and he is left with no alternative but to act for himself to gain the needed experience.

Törless's active search for his identity takes the form of experimentation with possibilities for self-realization. His notion that reality lies behind layers of masking superficiality leads him to the conclusion that he can only find himself by transcending to another realm in which the truth, including that of his own nature, becomes visible. The experiments that he conducts involve the exploration of potential doorways to that "Other Condition."

In contrast to the tangible world with which he is familiar, the object of his longing is a sphere of pure feeling. Yvon Desportes has argued that Musil's concept in this instance was influenced by his study of Ernst Mach's theories, and that in Mach's terminology the "Other Condition" corresponds to "a universe of pure ideas."[7]

The first door that Törless tries in his search for the passageway to his goal is that of his growing sexual awareness. Johannes Loebenstein has pointed out that Törless thinks he has found in sexuality an absolute bridge that has the potential to bind the two separate worlds together.[8] Sunday visits to the whore Božena become extremely important to him, not for sexual experience as such, but as a source of information about himself. Although the prostitute is powerless to unlock all of the forces that are building up inside him, she has enough femininity to call forth pieces of what lies dormant, waiting for the instant of complete realization. Thus, in his encounters with her, the boy obtains premature glimpses of a self that may emerge to full view in the future.

Törless's encounters with Božena fail to achieve the desired result primarily because he is unable to commit himself to a physical relationship. Aversion to the sex act itself and fear of its possible consequences keep him from immersing himself in sexual experience, with the result that just his imagination moves in an unhealthy direction. His mental processes then lead him to a dead end. They open only a world in which fulfillment remains forever out of reach. Within it he becomes a part of something that links Božena to his mother. In that context, everything else assumes a new, threatening, treacherous dimension. At the shock of the sudden awareness of his mother's sexuality, he can do nothing but retreat once more into his own isolation.

The possibility of finding refuge in separation from the everyday world attracts Törless into the environment where he faces his second major opportunity to open the way to the unknown realm. In an otherwise unused attic chamber, Reiting and Beineberg have established a private hideaway called the "red room" where they can pursue their special interests without interference from teachers or other representatives of the adult establishment. Törless joins them in their activities there, but his feelings toward the red room are ambivalent. While he is drawn by its constriction and isolation, his companions' superficial embellishments that are supposed to create an extreme illusion of rebellion and mystery seem ridiculous to him.

Wilfried Berghahn has interpreted the secret chamber as a symbol for "the truly horrible element" that "sits in the caverns beneath the surface" of the humane façade of modern times.[9] For Törless, however, it is a doorway to a more threatening kind of experience in the universe of feeling. In his thoughts he identifies it as a gate from the daylight world of his previous experience, into a different realm, where everything is hushed, yet seething with passion and destruction. His encounters in the attic are important because they make him conscious of the fact that he is really torn between two worlds. One of them is the concrete world of respectability and order in which he lived as a child at home. The other is the adventurous world of the unknown, a world that he mentally associates with darkness, blood, and mysteries.

Törless senses that the red room is a point of transfer to an extremely dangerous condition. During his initial visit, he is startled and disturbed by the fact that within its confines Reiting and Beineberg seem suddenly transformed from the people of the warm bright life in the schoolrooms into sinister, threatening figures that seem to belong to a different kind of life. Yet it is not the awareness of danger that prevents him from passing through this particular portal into the "Other Condition." Once again the critical factor is his inability to commit himself to action by making a firm choice between the possibilities that attract him. When he is faced with coming to a decision, with risking the acceptance of some possibility as probability and acting accordingly, he fails. Suddenly his interest is gone and he no longer has the energy to act.

There is a suggestion near the beginning of the novel that the knowledge of self, if obtained during the critical period of puberty, can be destructive. According to the narrator, the danger that exists during this particular period is such that if a boy is confronted with his own ridiculousness, he will lose his footing in reality and fall headlong, like a sleepwalker who awakens to find himself surrounded by nothing but empty air. In the example of Basini, Törless receives the opportunity to observe such a fall. The revelation of Basini's thefts rips away the facade that has hidden his true nature, gives him a different identity, and in so doing plunges him into the predicted abyss. As Törless analyzes what has happened, he recognizes that Basini, who was like himself only the day before, has undergone a sudden change as a result of his fall, a change that has turned him into someone else. In a sense, by thus exposing his deepest identity, Basini becomes an alien element in the larval world and is now vulnerable to the attacks of its other inhabitants.

Awareness of the pit into which he too may fall causes Törless to examine possibilities for crossing the void. His encounter with the imaginary numbers of mathematics is a key incident in his striving to build a bridge across the emptiness. It symbolizes his attempt to apply known principles of order in answering the question at hand. As he struggles to understand how the imaginary numbers are employed in solving problems, he describes to Beineberg the confusion that such ideas create for him.

For Törless, the problem lies in his inability to conceptualize a process that begins and ends with real numbers, yet moves from one set to another by means of something that does not exist. He compares what apparently transpires to the safe crossing of a bridge that has solid pilings at each end but nothing in the middle. Such a feat seems to contradict his knowledge of the real world, and he finds it extremely difficult to accept. Therefore, when something as fixed as mathematics begins to waver, signaling that the trusted constants of life cannot be relied upon for direction, the result for Törless is painful uncertainty and the experience of chaos.

Because he recognizes that Basini's confrontation with his own criminal nature has plunged him into the destructive abyss that threatens the seekers of the "Other Condition," Törless begins an experiment with the younger cadet's soul. The object is to learn what Basini felt while falling into the void. By "dissecting" Basini's soul, Törless hopes to find clues that will enable him to avoid the trapdoor that leads to the psychological emptiness where Basini now resides. Törless's inquiry is conducted simultaneously with the investigations of Reiting and Beineberg. Reiting uses

Basini to test his ideas about the political manipulation of people, while Beineberg subjects his victim to routines that are intended to reveal the manner of passage into the higher spiritual realm described by the Indian ascetics.

During the course of his experiment, Törless is troubled by the suspicion that what he is doing is meaningless, an idea that destroys his "scientific" concentration. Once his attention is broken, he becomes vulnerable to a sexual lure of a different kind than the one encountered with Božena. Basini is not bound by traditional forms of erotic behavior, and for that reason he temporarily becomes for Törless what Uwe Baur has termed "the embodiment of the 'other world' "[10] Like the earlier experience with the prostitute, however, the homosexual relationship with Basini fails to move Törless into the absolute realm of feeling. Törless is unable to commit himself to finding fulfillment in Basini's "love," and Basini cannot satisfy Törless's hunger for the unattainable. Although something like passion arises within him, Törless's response is purely physical, and Basini becomes a superficial surrogate for the object of a much deeper longing. The only real effect that Basini has on the other boy is to magnify his desire into something that extends far beyond anything that this specific relationship can provide.

The collapse of the experiment causes Törless to abandon the search for external doors to the "Other Condition." When Beineberg and Reiting insist that he watch their punishment of Basini for requesting that Törless intervene with them in his behalf, Törless refuses. Where he had previously been seeking the hidden meaning behind their acts, he can now see only the vulgarity and brutality of his two companions.

At numerous points along his course, Törless has been given clues to the direction that he must take in order to gain the desired knowledge about himself. One of the strongest hints is given by Beineberg, who insists that real human beings are the only ones who are able to penetrate to their own inner selves through meditation that unfolds their relationship to the eternal processes of the universe. According to Beineberg, these individuals have the ability to perform miracles with ease because they understand how to use all of the forces of the universe, forces that exist both within and outside of them. Proceeding from this perception of man's nature, he then suggests that only the person who is able to see his own soul completely is capable of entering a higher plane of existence.

In another instance Törless briefly grasps the fact that his struggle with mathematical concepts is pointing him inward. When he tries to explain his confusion to Beineberg, he says that the torment that mathematics has given him comes from the fact that he seeks something different behind it than others do. What he is looking for is not supernatural, but natural, not outside him, but within him. And nevertheless, it is something that he does not understand.

Viewed in that light, the failure of Törless's attempts to enter the world of feeling, either through sensual experience or through the Basini experiment, becomes a catalyst that forces him to take the only way that remains open to him. While examining his setbacks, he comes to the understanding that he has followed an elusive phantom along a path that leads deep inside himself. In the process of this quest he has grown weary. The inescapable conclusion is that access to his own identity is not hidden beneath the surface of other people and things. Rather, it is within himself. With that knowledge he is finally prepared to solve the mystery of his own nature.

Throughout his stay at the academy, Törless struggles with what he perceives as the duality of existence. Looking back on his life, he says that he sees everything, including ideas, in two different ways. He even remembers a time in his childhood when he had seen himself in a second form, as a girl.[11] It is the idea of doubleness that causes him to seek his identity in an alternate plane, when his initial examination of self yields only a vision of emptiness. The discovery that the world of his identity lies within him forces him to recognize that what he has interpreted as a second, more authentic manifestation of a scrutinized object is in fact an image created by an inner part of himself. This other aspect of his being observes and gives life to its surroundings from a different perspective. In defending the new view of himself that he has gained from his experience, he insists that he was correct in his speculation that things have a mysterious second existence that nobody notices. It is not a literal life as such, but rather a subjective state of being that is discerned only by an individual such as Törless who examines things with eyes other than those of reason.

The comprehension of the split that exists within him is the essence of Törless's final discovery of himself. In a letter to his friend Stefanie Tyrka, Musil described the inner nature of his young protagonist in these words: "The ego is literally divided. It attains a double footing, and through the clouded glasses of the first and hitherto only one, one sees mysterious motions without being able to interpret them."

Acceptance of his own duality enables Törless to resolve the conflicts that have troubled him and to face the future with a firm grasp on his position in it. His words to the men who investigate the Basini affair confirm that he is now prepared to enter the realm of adult reality. Although he acknowledges that reality will probably retain its existing characteristics, and that he will continue to see these properties at times from the perspective of reason, and at other times subjectively, he insists that he has reached the point where he will never again compare the two views with one another.

3

~~~~~~

Looking Inside: *Unions*

An important distinguishing feature of Musil's literary art is the deliberate de-emphasis of structured plot and sequential narrative in favor of illustrating and illuminating his ideas about mortal existence. Characters and their relationships become the vehicles that the author uses to explore theme variations and possibilities for response to the phenomena, problems, and questions of human life. In the slender volume *Unions*, which contains the two novellas *The Perfecting of a Love* and *The Temptation of Quiet Veronica*, Musil experimented with a creative technique that pushed to a new extreme the development of this tendency in his writings. Focusing almost completely on the thoughts and feelings of the respective female protagonists, he subordinated any sense of story line and perspective to a precise rendering of their inner worlds in a dense, carefully constructed web of metaphors. The resulting literature is extremely complex and difficult to understand. Musil himself suggested that in order to appreciate the stories, the reader should contemplate and ponder them like pieces of visual art. His diary reveals that he regarded *Unions* as something entirely different from traditional narrative prose, something that could best be understood by removing it from any association with the concept: "book." He felt that the stories would better communicate their meaning if they were separated into pages that could be placed on display under glass and exchanged at appropriate intervals.

The style of *Unions* is abstract and lyrical. There is a pronounced absence of real specifics concerning time and place. The physical world is often subdued and shadowy or excluded entirely. Instead of a connected flow of events, the narrative substance consists mainly of floods of thought, surges of emotion, and intense projections of feelings and sensations. Musil consciously associated the two novellas with the poetry of ideas, and the heavy fabric of metaphors and images forces the reader to approach these writings from precisely that kind of perspective. In a letter to Franz Blei, Musil pointed out that his usage of stylistic devices in *Unions,* especially symbolic and parabolic forms of expression, deviated from the norm. He insisted that such components of his writing were not secondary, decorative trappings, but rather primary aspects of the narrative and critical elements of its structure.

The overall effect of this approach is very poetic, and the lyrical aspect contributes directly to the penetration of the protagonists' inner worlds, or, as Musil termed it, "the boring into the psychological dimension" that is the author's major purpose.[1] Eithne Wilkins and Ernst Kaiser have accurately summed up the role of lyricism in *Unions* as follows: "Through the lyrical element there arises in these novellas a greater density of symbols than is present in the more discursive works, but these too are full of suggestions of new, still half-hidden horizons of consciousness, of indications of a boundary and what lies mysteriously behind it, of that which is extreme and the borderline case."[2]

In addition to the stylistic density of the novellas, the obscurity of Musil's primary focus contributes to the difficulty that is typically encountered in the attempt to interpret *Unions.* Experience with traditional narrative prose, in which relationships between characters carry much of the story weight, tempts the reader to relate the volume's title to the establishment and failure of connections between portrayed individuals and to seek in that equation the central meanings of the respective stories. Musil's own comments indicate that such an interpretation must lead to misunderstanding of his intent. The "unions" that are important take place *within* the protagonists, and the author is more concerned with the devaluation of all causality, and with the problems of self-betrayal and the relationship of the individual to his ideals than with the ties between his heroines and the men in their lives.

The first of the narratives in *Unions, The Perfecting of a Love*, lays bare the inner life of Claudine, a woman whose physical trip to visit her daughter at a boarding school in an isolated town provides the external guideposts for a parallel voyage into the depths of her own soul. The outward happenings of the story are minimal. After leaving her husband alone, Claudine takes the train to the city where her daughter is studying and there eventually allows herself to be seduced by a man who remains a stranger. Paradoxically, she seems to experience her unfaithfulness as a process of perfecting her love for her husband, and what transpires within her during the period of her separation from him forms the real substance of the novella.

As was the case with the main character of *Young Törless*, the point of departure for Claudine's journey into herself is a potent tension that arises from an increasing sense of spiritual isolation. The opening scene of *The Perfecting of a Love*, which is peculiar for its intensity of concrete detail, invokes a feeling of loneliness on several levels at once. Claudine and her husband sit drinking tea as though suspended in what Frederick Peters has described as "an impressionistic painting, a still life of fruits and flowers or lifeless puppets rather than of two human beings."[3] There is an immediate sense of something at once beautiful and fragile that cannot survive outside of the hermetically closed sphere in which it now exists.

Conversation between husband and wife, and the author's representation of their thoughts, intensify the mood of separation from the world that is evoked by the rich but sterile minutiae of their environment. The focus of their discussion is a sexual deviant about whom they have been reading. Like some peculiar apparition, the man identified only as G. haunts their thoughts and stimulates consciousness of their personal isolation. Their contemplation of the criminal, his deeds, and motivations leads unerringly to the concluding question: "Yes indeed, isn't every mind solitary?" The response to the query is only silence, a signal to the reader that the focus has shifted away from G. and back to the people who are thinking about him, and the result is an overwhelmingly cold, harsh impression of intense isolation. It is then from this perspective of loneliness that the nature of Claudine's actual relationship with her husband is revealed.

The two characters are described as feeling that the secret of their union rests upon the solitude that they experience. Their vision of the surrounding world is almost opaque, a fact that makes them seem to cling to one another. With a sense of coldness around them, they derive warmth from the peculiar joining of one to the other that forces them internally into a larger whole. Although aloneness has brought the two of them together, their relationship is flawed because they remain unable to perfect their union on any external plane. Proceeding from that state of affairs, Claudine's journey quickly transforms itself into the search for an alternative solution to the problem, within herself.

The physical events that occur after Claudine leaves home represent an intensification of her isolation in both time and space. The time element is especially important. In the description of her departure there is an immediate shift in narrative focus from Claudine's present to her past, and the greatest emphasis is given to things that contributed to an earlier sense of separation from everything around her. As she waits at the railway station, she remembers when she experienced passionate acts that virtually humiliated her because of their violence, even though she remained continually aware that nothing she did really had any important impact upon her or meaning for her life. Her memory is then juxtaposed with the present in which she feels uneasy about the people around her and is moved to seek refuge within herself. Once she is on the train, its soft rocking movements and the view of nature passing outside the window enable her to com-

plete her escape into solitude. Subsequently, when elements of
the external world threaten to intrude and the people around her
begin to touch her thoughts, she is able to retreat without difficulty
into an inner place where she is left only with a feeling of her
own insignificance that causes her to drift within herself toward
an indefinite goal. By the time she reaches the city where her
daughter is, her mood is such that she views the town itself as
cut off from reality, and she is prepared for the encounter that
will enable her to reach her goal. Her readiness is signaled by an
inexpressible yearning for some man who is as misunderstood
and lonely as she is. Such an individual, she believes, would be
characterized by a tenderness that would have the power to subdue
the external, material world, while maintaining the perfect security of the inner, spiritual realm through a balanced consciousness of the self. Clearly, what she yearns for is union with her
own deepest being.

    Claudine's encounter with the isolated boarding-school town
is like Törless's stay at the academy in that her interpretations of
events are colored and confused by an awareness of the world's
apparent doubleness. At one point the narrator says that each
thing she sees appears to illuminate surrounding things in a re-
ciprocal manner that makes them appear to echo one another in
a broader pattern of vision. Frederick Peters relates this phenomenon more closely to the kind of search for identity that Musil
described in his first novel by arguing that the city "functions as
a geographical metaphor for the Other Realm that lies beyond
the frontier of everyday life."[4]

    Claudine's experience differs from that of Törless, however,
because her perception of duplication is primarily temporal rather
than spatial. Even the "echo" metaphor cited above places the
emphasis on repetition in *time*. For Claudine, the "Other Realm"
is the past. All of her experiences seem to be repetitions of earlier
ones, and even her words have the ring of things that she has
spoken previously. Accordingly, her entry into the internal world
where the union with self can be perfected is tied to her return

to the former spiritual state in which she can perform again acts of physical passion that have no real effect on her.

Critics who interpret what happens to Claudine as a true perfecting of her love for her husband overlook the fact that on a real plane, union with him, even a spiritual one, and the return to the past are mutually exclusive.[5] It is the physical and mental separation from her husband that permits her to slide back into her former life, while dwelling in that past brings a sadness that she cannot associate with a normal longing for love. On the contrary, the feeling within her seems to move her away from the intense relationship with her husband in the real world, and toward some other, as yet indistinguishable goal. The impression that she has is one of being on a road to a particularly sublime loneliness in which she is exposed to the harsh elements of an empty wasteland.

Alone in her room after her arrival, Claudine is engulfed by dreams from her early life. There she recognizes that she is not attracted to the stranger that she has been watching, but only by the intense anticipation of the ecstasy that she will experience in the confrontation with her own deepest being. In that moment of longing for self she has a premonition of the "mysterious union" that is coming, and it is again connected with an image that emphasizes distance from rather than proximity to her loved one. The narrator presents it as an act of hearing the distant, restless, homeless wandering of her husband's heart. The sounds that her spirit detects form a strange kind of flickering music that touches her with a profound sense of loneliness, and the loneliness in turn becomes a catalyst that enables her to transcend the former limits of her soul.

Like Törless, Claudine discovers the duality of her own nature by peering into the "Other Realm." The aspect belonging to the world from which she has come is the ideal Claudine that cannot live without the mate she has left behind. During her return to the past, however, she is dominated by another, baser, more sensual self that the author presents in animalistic metaphors. During the night, for example, she wakes up and goes to the window to look out at the falling snow. She is described specifically as being keenly aware that her feet touch the ground like those of some animal.

The confrontation with her animal self becomes more intense with each incident that takes place. At the boarding school, when she talks with the teachers about her daughter (who is a product of a disinterested physical-animal act in her promiscuous past), she experiences a strange but meaningful vision in which a peculiar something seems to rise from the shadows, confronting her with the impression of a huge, shaggy, evil-smelling beast. Her initial inclination to lash out at it and drive it away is destroyed by a sudden realization: The changing expressions on the apparition's face are extremely familiar; in some unknown fashion they mirror her own.

This encounter with the animal side of her being is the turning point in the narrative. Its effect on her is extremely powerful. Immediately afterward she attempts to envision her husband, with the result that she can no longer see him as clearly or as near to her as before. It is at that point that she considers a variety of possibilities for action and concludes that the spiritual merging with her husband can only be consummated *within herself* when all external events become meaningless. In that context, the physical attraction that she has for the nameless official who has been trying to win her favor provides the opportunity for her to achieve the perfect union that she desires.

The civil servant becomes an outward symbol for her animal self, and her intended sexual submission to him without emotional involvement, the ultimate proof of her accomplishment, is equated in her mind with sodomy. Her subsequent mental behavior then emphasizes the increasing dominance of the animal element within her. On the night when her potential seducer remains outside her door without knocking, she later looks out into the empty hallway and responds silently to what has happened. In presenting what takes place within her, the narrator describes her sudden impulse to throw herself to the ground and kiss the footprints on the rug, comparing this feeling of arousal to the animal actions of a bitch in heat.

When the stranger finally follows her to her room, the author again transforms her metaphorically into an animal. Upon hearing his footsteps on the stairs behind her, she mentally distances herself from what is happening, while her physical reaction is to tremble "like an animal hunted down, deep in the forest." On that level she surrenders to him. For Claudine, the stranger too is an animal, but without identity. As Frederick Peters has pointed out, "a particular man with a particular history . . . could not have conquered her."[6]

The major metaphors that form the skeleton of *The Perfecting of a Love* suggest a variety of possibilities for union on different levels, ranging from disinterested or totally submissive mechanical coupling to intensely spiritual unification. While the animal metaphors are the most graphic of these, the most important ones pertain to Claudine's perception of her relationship to her distant husband. Her peculiar notion that the sexual affair with a stranger will mysteriously enable her to perfect the marital bond is a troublesome problem that can be resolved only through recognition that the love tie itself is but a metaphor for something else. That fact becomes clear in the progression of thoughts that builds to a critical climax during the night that Claudine spends away from the civil servant.

What happens to Claudine in her room is prefigured in a train of thought that she entertains while sitting with the stranger before going upstairs. The temptation to submit herself to him causes her to project a mental image of a union in which her spirit disowns and abandons her body, leaving it open to the physical, sensual, even murderous assaults of the stranger, while at the same time experiencing the constancy of her physical being as an enduring presence around the soul that she can only define as a sickness. Like Törless, she is looking for a means to make contact with her deepest essence.

The experience that occurs when she is alone is generated

not by her love for her husband but by her overt denial of it. During her conversation with the stranger, he had asked her whether she loved her husband, and she had given a negative response. As she ponders the significance of this lie, it becomes for her a gateway to the "Other Realm," a place where she is no longer subject to the binding force of her ideals.

While sitting in her room, anticipating the adventure in which she will commit adultery and yet remain somehow aloof from the act, she feels a dangerous excitement that she associates with the very concept of betraying her husband. This feeling enables her to transcend the limits of physical reality. Spiritually, she moves into a state in which her soul is beyond the reach of other people. The narrator describes this ethereal domain as "the void that sometimes gapes for an instant behind all ideals." Once the door to this place of total isolation has been opened, her mind can lead her to the fulfillment that she seeks.

The moment of perfection comes neither in sexual union with the stranger nor in the envisioned spiritual joining with her husband, but in the achievement of oneness within herself. Musil describes it as an instant of closing up the soul against all foreign elements. Perfection is realized in a dreamlike state where the contradictions of life are dissolved in the trembling light of an intense and undefiled love. Viewed from this perspective, the subsequent sexual affair with the civil servant becomes an anticlimax that verifies only her attainment of a state of internal harmony that renders physical entanglements completely meaningless.

Like Claudine, the central figure of *The Temptation of Quiet Veronica* searches for a means to become one with her innermost self. For Veronica, the process of realizing internal unity involves the rejection of normal sexual activity in the belief that she can reach a more significant relationship with her friend Johannes on a higher, more spiritual plane. The focal event of her quest is a peculiar, semimystical experience that leads only briefly to perfect oneness because it cannot be sustained in the real world.

The Temptation of Quiet Veronica has been called Musil's

most abstract narrative, primarily because of its lack of any substantial realistic story line.[7] While the literary presentation develops the relationships between three main characters who live together in an old house, aside from opaque conversations and descriptions of a few minor happenings, the only external action is Johannes's departure by train for the coast, followed a day later by the arrival of a letter from him containing the news that he has not committed suicide as Veronica expected him to do. Everything else that is offered for the reader's examination occurs within the characters, primarily Veronica, with no more than general, indefinite reference to factors of time and space.

In many respects, *The Temptation of Quiet Veronica* offers an intensification of the central themes in *The Perfecting of a Love*. Once more the point of departure for the female protagonist's excursion into the uttermost recesses of her soul is a profound state of spiritual aloneness. Musil's employment of the house's indistinct, almost timeless, realm as a metaphor for separation from reality is particularly powerful. It is, in the words of Frederick Peters, "as if three people were each living in complete isolation in a shadowy dreamlike world at the still bottom of a deep pool of water. They seem to wander about the house in varying states of agonized emotional tension, now and then engaging in elliptical conversations as they glide past each other."[8]

The most visible symptom of the insulating void that exists between the major figures is their inability to communicate effectively to each other their thoughts and feelings. Musil conveys the spoken word's failure to bring about interpersonal union by presenting as conversation what seem to be random pieces of monologues that never go anywhere. By this means he forces the reader into the stream-of-consciousness pattern that leads in a sequence of complex metaphors into the inner world of his central character.

Critical factors in Veronica's failure to participate in normal human interaction are the pronounced tensions that exist between her and the two male figures Johannes and Demeter. Strong parallels are visible between the respective relationships and the corresponding elements that permit different aspects of Claudine's nature to respond to her husband and to the unnamed civil servant in *The Perfecting of a Love*. In each of the Veronica situations, however, the strain placed on ties between individuals and the metaphors that represent those connections are more extreme than those of the first novella.

For Claudine, the physical separation of the train trip combined with her mental retreat into the past place enough distance between her and her husband to enable her to "perfect" her love by transcending its bonds and achieving unity within herself. In the case of Veronica, a far more drastic parting is necessary for her to find what she is seeking. Johannes suggests to her that they leave the house and go away together in order to find a common focus around which they can join their lives. Veronica rejects his proposal, and when he renews it she responds in words that define both her perception of him and the only circumstances under which she can envision union between them on any level. She says: "Surely no human being can be so impersonal, only an animal . . . yes, perhaps if you were going to die." The real reason why Veronica cannot accept Johannes on his terms is that she sees him as an animal. Only through the complete destruction of that image, that is, only through his death, can he become something with which she can possibly unite on a mystical plane.

In *The Perfecting of a Love* Musil employs the animal metaphors most pointedly to depict and highlight Claudine's perception of the stranger and her approach to the sexual encounter with him. Vivid symbols of the same kind are used to characterize the relationship between Veronica and Demeter.

Like the civil servant, Demeter represents mechanical, completely physical intercourse that has no meaning. After Demeter has made a sexual proposition to her, Veronica tells Johannes about it. Her description reveals the lack of significance that such an act would have for either her or Demeter. She presents what happened as a natural, mechanical event, a deed that was meaningless, according to Demeter, because nobody would know about it, and it would therefore have no relationship to things in the external world of reality. To emphasize the incident's triviality, she concludes by insisting that Demeter meant nothing at all to her.

Although Veronica does not feel anything *for* Demeter, he does have a powerful impact upon her that is conditioned by her tendency to relate him to specific animal images. At one point, for example, as she watches the chickens in the yard beneath the window, she senses that she has been thinking about something that she cannot identify. Demeter comes and stands next to her and his presence acts as a catalyst that brings her elusive thought into focus. She has been thinking about the rooster below. While relating the incident to Johannes, she tells him how the thought suddenly came to her that Demeter must be like the rooster.

In his diary Musil wrote that he originally intended to present Veronica as a figure caught between two antagonistic tendencies, the sensuality that dominated her thoughts, and an internal longing for balance. Demeter and Johannes are the respective external stimuli that alternately focus her awareness on the two forces that struggle within her and through their conflict make it impossible for her to reach a permanent internal harmony. Each represents a temptation that must be faced if Veronica is to come to grips with her own destiny.

Frederick Peters has argued that Veronica's awareness of Demeter's animal essence, in the scene where she relates him to the rooster, is a primary "precipitating agent" for the return of a repressed sexual memory that explains why she rejects his physical advances.[9] While it is certainly true that what she finally brings herself to recall holds the key to the tension that she feels with respect to sexual activity, there is no clear causal relationship in the text between the rooster scene and the regeneration of the memory that occurs several pages later. The attempt to link the two events so closely places a false emphasis on the relationship between Veronica and Demeter. What is important about the

sudden awakening within her of the experience from her childhood is that it explains why she can unite with *neither* Johannes
nor Demeter in the real world.

As Veronica attempts to deal with her internal conflict, she
goes through a process that corresponds to Claudine's retreat into
the past. Over a period of weeks she is deluged with mental pictures from her early life. The direct stimulus for the final critical
memory is an exchange of calls by two birds, and it seems to
Veronica in retrospect that similar birdcalls have heralded the
other flashes of remembrance. At the sound of the birds' song,
Veronica suddenly sees a time when she had loved the fur of a
large Saint Bernard dog. On a particular day, as she lies beside
the dog, her mind roams through peculiar fantasies with sexual
overtones. She closes her eyes for a while, and when she opens
them again, the dog is looking at her. At this point she becomes
aware of the dog's sexual arousal, as she catches sight of its penis
protruding from the fur. When she tries to get up, the dog licks
her face, and she is unable to move. It is as though she is an
animal herself, and emotionally she struggles between her fears
concerning what is happening and some peculiar feeling of ecstasy
that she does not understand.

The meaning of this vision of the past for Veronica's attitudes
toward Johannes and Demeter is vividly clear. For years she has
carried within her the suppressed knowledge of an experience
that has in effect reduced her to an animal at the sexual mercy
of a large dog. Her mental association of Johannes and Demeter
with various animal images, including dogs, creates an unconscious equation of their relationships with what has transpired
when she was a teenager. For that reason she is totally incapable
of submitting to the real-world desires of either male figure. With
respect to Johannes in particular, that fact is hammered home
in a mental association in which she relates him directly to the
dog of her memory. As she feels the intensity of his gaze resting
upon her, within her mind he assumes the characteristics of a
large exhausted animal that is lying on her, and that she cannot

push away. This association calls forth again the vision of that afternoon in her past. In the act of mentally reliving the traumatic event from her youth, she overcomes it and opens the way for her brief encounter with inner oneness.

After Johannes departs by train for the coast, where, Veronica believes, he will commit suicide, she returns to her room and retreats into an internal world where she contemplates the possibility of achieving union with him on a mystical plane. There the souls would become joined in a fashion that is impossible in the realm of physical reality. In the process of her examination of that prospect, her sense of ecstasy intensifies. She seems to wallow in the vision of Johannes's impending death and in her own yearning to unite with his soul. As the intensity of feeling increases, however, she experiences the revelation of what really lies at the heart of her innermost longing: "She had begun dimly to realise that it was not Johannes but herself that she experienced with such palpable sensuality."

What follows is the enjoyment of what Frederick Peters has called "the moment of ultimate narcissism."[10] Suddenly Johannes loses importance as a being in his own right. He becomes a vehicle for Veronica's observation of herself. A mystical union of souls occurs in which she penetrates beyond the physical trappings of her body into the innermost reaches of herself. She seems to see herself through Johannes's eyes, and to experience not only his spiritual touch but also his sense of contact with her.

The semimystical experience that permits Veronica to become one with her own soul brings about the same kind of resolution of the basic problems of insecurity and spiritual loneliness that Claudine achieves. The union with self that results from the attempt to "perfect a love" demands in the real world a rejection of that love. Complete oneness with the soul and an emotional tie to another individual are mutually exclusive because, as Veronica learns, it is the soul of living people that makes them unable to love, regardless of how much they may yearn to do so.

When Veronica learns that Johannes is still alive, the news

destroys any hope that she might have of maintaining the state of inner unity that she has achieved the night before. Her mental vision of his death was a necessary bridge to the "Other Realm" in which the union could occur. Without it, her endeavors to regain what she has experienced cause her to drift into the void between the reality from which she has excluded herself and the transcendent world that she can no longer reach. From physical isolation in the old house, she has moved into the devastating loneliness of mental illness, a realm where there is "perhaps only a sadness . . . like walls painted by fever and delusions, and between those walls the words spoken by the sane and healthy have no resonance, but fall to the ground, meaningless. . . . "

4

A Sense of Possibility:
Two Dramas

In a journal entry written while he was working on *Unions*, Musil defined literature as "a more daringly, more logically combined life, a production or an analysis of possibilities." As his literary career progressed, each succeeding creation became a more refined exploration of the varying prospects for human experience, especially with respect to the problems of self-discovery and self-definition. The postwar works reflect the author's ever-increasing interest in protagonists who have what he called a "sense of possibility." For Musil, this awareness of the unfixed nature of things sets the creative individual apart from the rest of the world.

Musil viewed his own writings as illustrations of art's mutability in its symbolic representation of specific ideas. While the ideas themselves are the essence of the literary product, the symbols, characters, and situations employed to communicate them remain interchangeable and have no intrinsic value of their own. They are important only as ideographs, an element that Musil felt was missing from expressionist drama, that he accordingly rejected as an unsuitable pattern for his own work.

The content and genesis of his first play, *The Enthusiasts* (also translated as *The Visionaries*), offer particularly vivid examples of how Musil applied the principle of variability to the creative process. Not only does the drama focus concretely upon the tension between possibility and reality, but it actually *is* only one alternative among others that Musil envisioned as potential vehicles for conveying his message. Before choosing the final framework for *The Enthusiasts*, he actually created three different versions of the play with alternate plots, scenarios, and character groupings.

The rendering that Musil selected offers new variations on notions and themes that he treated in earlier writings. There are especially interesting connections between *The Enthusiasts* and *The Temptation of Quiet Veronica*. In addition to the similar settings in large old houses that seem cut off from the outside world, parallels between characters and specific personal and interpersonal problems are particularly visible. A major focus of *The Enthusiasts*, for example, involves projection of an alternative development of the Veronica-Johannes scenario from *The Temptation of Quiet Veronica*. In the new configuration, Johannes does commit suicide instead of escaping into the realm of reality. Further, Musil's characteristic preoccupation with questions of individual isolation, circumstances that may promote union, the "Other Condition" and its relationship to the past and childhood, failure of communication, and the culmination of the search for identity in recognition of the dual nature of personality, shapes important aspects of the play.

The resulting creation is an intense exploration of ideas for their own sake. It de-emphasizes traditional dramatic action. A pronounced heaviness in this respect has been a major factor in its historical lack of popularity in the theater. Although a few somewhat successful productions were offered to the public after 1950, no truly effective visual presentation of the material was achieved until 1984, when Hans Neuenfels employed modern film techniques to approach *The Enthusiasts* from a totally new perspective.

Hellmuth Karasek suggests in his review of the film that Neuenfels "violates" *The Enthusiasts*,[1] and indeed there are substantial differences between his rendition and Musil's original. Nevertheless, with its exposure of the characters' internal worlds,

its artistic treatment of symbols, dreams, and possibilities of experience, its tone and generation of mood, the motion picture
perhaps comes closer to the spirit of Musil's work than does any
earlier live performance.

Musil's primary concern in *The Enthusiasts* is the portrayal
of characters who represent different options for coming to grips
with what Sibylle Bauer has called "the possibility of realizing
true human identity and preserving it unadulterated."[2] These figures live in an unfinished world and are themselves subject to
change and variation, with the result that they remain unclear
and in some respects indefinite. Although the inner dramatic
tension of the piece arises out of the conflict between positions
of idealism and realism, none of the major participants consistently represents either view of the world. As Günther Schneider
has pointed out: "It is characteristic for Musil's play that the
idealistic position and the cynical antiposition are not distributed
among the different persons as firm roles. All characters assume
in constant alternation sometimes the part of the idealist, sometimes the part of the realist."[3]

The author's insistence on variability and lack of final definition in the dramatis personae results in a corresponding fluidity
of the world that is presented in the play. Each situation offers
some sort of plurality of alternatives that promotes a constant
rearranging of relationships, comparisons, and symbols. Causal
connections lose their rigidity, and fixed reality is replaced by
possibilities that have the weight of established facts with respect
to individual lives. Accordingly, it is the mental-spiritual process
of coping with the variables of experience, rather than the traditional progress of action toward a final resolution of conflicts,
that forms the essence of the drama.

As the characters struggle mentally with problems related to
identity, self-assertion, their own motivation for action, deter-
mination of values, and the possibility of communication, they
introduce the audience to the dramatist's key ideas. This occurs
within the framework of what is characterized by one of Musil's

critics as "a trite and typical plot, often repeated and well-known both in life and on the stage. In the play it is a story of adultery with a double triangle constellation presented as a family scandal. The story line corresponds to what is typical for a normal kitchen-sink drama."[4]

The external course of events is a product of interaction among four primary and three secondary figures. In a large country house, Thomas, a successful scholar, and his wife Maria are visited by Maria's sister, Regine, and Regine's lover, Anselm, an old friend of Thomas. Regine is married to Josef, her second husband. She is still struggling emotionally with the death of her first husband, Johannes, who committed suicide in the same house years earlier. Anselm, a ne'er-do-well adventurer, has persuaded Regine and her companion, Miss Mertens, to leave Josef and flee to Thomas's house. There, however, Anselm devotes himself entirely to a relationship with Maria. Meanwhile, Josef has employed the detective Stader to investigate Anselm's past. With Stader's help, Thomas and Josef expose Anselm as a liar and rogue who is married, yet chases other women and repeatedly betrays them. Anselm leaves; Maria decides to follow him in spite of the revelations about his character. When Josef learns that Regine is not the innocent creature that he has envisioned, specifically that she was sexually promiscuous during her first marriage, he also departs, followed by Miss Mertens, who is filled with moral indignation. Regine and Thomas remain alone in the house, where they try in vain to establish a relationship.

Musil couched within the above framework the interpersonal confrontations that permit many-sided discussion and exploration of the broader issues that were his real concern. By using creative techniques that he had previously tested in his prose, he established a second level of presentation, an almost essayistic aspect in which the dialogues become "less conversations *in* a dramatic happening, and more conversations *about* the dramatic conflicts that are interpreted and finally traced back to the conflict, the antinomy in the ideas."[5]

In writing *The Enthusiasts*, Musil employed a variety of stylistic devices to intensify the focus on major ideas. Among these features are carefully orchestrated language that places heavy demands on the actors,[6] repetition of aphoristic passages, and the typical emphasis on metaphors. The tension between reality and possibility is maintained through frequent use of the subjunctive mood.

Dialogues reflect the problems of communication in that figures often talk past one another. The characters themselves recognize this fact, even discuss it, but are unable to alter the situation. Thomas, for example, says to Anselm at one point that they are talking at cross-purposes. Both of them say the same things, he insists, but the perspectives are different. Carried to the extreme, this phenomenon results in scenes where it appears that monologues are presented next to each other.

The different levels at which internal problems of individuals are confronted find reflection in the presence of at least three kinds of conversation: discussion of concrete facts and relationships, projections of feeling and emotion, and rational argumentation and interpretation of questions pertaining to fundamental matters of proper human existence. It is the interchange of all of these elements that gives substance to the characters while maintaining their variability as symbols for modern middle-class life itself.

A number of critics have interpreted the four primary characters in *The Enthusiasts* as aspects of a single person, their creator. Günther Schneider, for example, points to the connection between Anselm, Regine, and Thomas and the different tasks that the dramatist performs: the selection of roles, the creation of a fictional world, and the critically analyzed transmission of ideas.[7] Such an interpretation has validity to the extent that the figures actually represent Musil in their presentation and treatment of vital questions concerning the nature and value of human existence.

The figure who corresponds most directly to Musil is the

scholar and scientist Thomas. Sibylle Bauer insists that he is the most important of the dramatis personae, describing his function in the play in these words: "He probably stands in the center most of all because he is least caught up in concrete reality, because he is the strongest interpreter of the situations, and because he strives especially to promote intellectual discussion with the others."[8] In his observations about himself, his friends, and life in general, Thomas focuses audience attention on most of the key issues with which Musil was concerned.

Thomas's analysis of the world and its relationships emphasizes the distinction between creative and noncreative individuals, between people who recognize and accept life as a diversity of possibilities, and others who are trapped within their own concepts of fixed reality. At one point while talking to Maria, he divides people into two groups, those who are only aware of what could be, and those who focus on things as they are. Members of the first group, he insists, have within them the potential for movement and change, while the people in the second are fixed. It is the ability to sense that things could be different, a quality found only in those who are not bound by reality, that is most attractive to Thomas. He views it as opening the door to endless possibilities for new experience.

For Thomas the very essence of a valid definition of what is truly human is the attribute of creative possibility, something that in their youth he, Anselm, and Johannes had possessed in all its power. His search for the right form of existence is therefore a constant effort to maintain the sense of possibility. As he describes his feelings at one point, he wants to preserve the illusion of walking through some unknown city where tremendous possibilities are still waiting for him. Because he focuses on possibility rather than reality, individuals and events become interchangeable, love for a selected individual is "nothing but aversion to everyone else," conventional middle-class moral perceptions are filled with contradictions, and truth and reality are swallowed up by "the abyss of mute loneliness."

Within Thomas's worldview, isolation is the characteristic condition of the true human being, the dreamer, the creative individual. Ironically, it is that very aloneness, a result of his cold and calculating personality, that makes Thomas himself seem so inhuman. In speaking to Maria about Thomas, Anselm insists that someone who is really human cannot isolate himself in a private configuration of thoughts, as Thomas does. For Anselm, the basic need to be with others, to be loved and encouraged, is the fundamental essence of being human. Without that need the individual lacks direction and purpose. Anselm's assessment of Thomas anticipates the direction in which the latter character's thinking will lead him. As Sibylle Bauer has concluded: "In his reflections Thomas does not achieve tangible goals, but rather the discovery and evaluation of potentialities, of forces of spontaneity."[9]

While Thomas functions primarily as a passive observer and interpreter of his surroundings, Regine, his female counterpart, employs her creative sense of possibility to isolate herself spiritually in a world beyond reality. Like Thomas, she views life as a process of choosing a course of action from among alternatives. In describing her position to Miss Mertens, she says that each individual enters the world with the potential to have even the most unspeakable kinds of experience. At first the laws do not bind the person, but ultimately he or she is forced to choose between two possibilities. What is most important for Regine, however, is the fact that when such choices must be made, there is always something missing, a third possibility without which the individual makes a choice but never achieves what is really desired. This sense of having missed better prospects as the result of her earlier choices is the basis for her attempts to escape from reality into a world of fantasy where she can reclaim lost opportunities.

The general direction of her flight from reality is into the past. On one level she, like the other enthusiasts, tries to recapture and maintain a state of being in which the potentialities of childhood remain accessible. Günther Schneider has outlined her purpose in doing so by saying that as an adult she still attempts to inhabit the world of her childhood, a world that transcends reality in scope, because the child remains unable to separate the realms of objective and subjective perception, or of reality and imagination. [10] In a broader sense, she is attempting to return to a time of expanded possibility, a time when experiences in the real world lose their importance when compared with what *might* happen.

Regine's most visible attempt to retreat into an earlier world of possibility is reflected in her peculiar mental-emotional relationship to the dead Johannes. While Johannes was alive, she had first denied him her sexual favors, insisting that she wanted to love him like a sister. Then, like Claudine in "The Perfecting of a Love," she had sought to "perfect" the relationship with her husband vicariously through sexual affairs with other men. Now, however, since his suicide, Johannes has become, as her husband Josef observes, a symbol for what she really wanted to become, a faith in herself, a vision of freedom from temporal and material restraints.

Like quiet Veronica, whose anticipation of her Johannes's death leads her to temporary fulfillment in the *thought* of a new mystical union with him, Regine enters the "Other Condition" through her worship of Johannes as an idea that permits her to do anything she wishes. From that perspective, love for the dead Johannes becomes for Regine a viable alternative to the love for living people that she cannot realize because she finds it impossible to love them when she can see what they really are.

Thomas and Regine follow paths that are determined by their belief in the creative power of possibility. For Anselm and Maria, a different outcome results from the failure of the sense of possibility to preserve the illusions under which they have conducted their lives. Instead of isolating themselves in realms of idea or fantasy beyond the here and now, they ultimately retreat into reality, thereby following a course opposite to that of Thomas and Regine.

At the beginning of the play, Anselm is an active player of roles whose life is a constant jumping from one prospect to another. He acts out various parts because he needs people to believe in him. At the same time, the various façades that he assumes symbolize a deep inner longing for true freedom of action and mutability of existence. Günther Schneider says: "Lies instead of truth, fraud instead of accomplishment, theater instead of life seem on the one hand to be cowardice and flight, on the other, however, also expression of a rejection of reality, a yearning to be different and changeable, and to be attempts not only to experience but also to live, not only to have but also to be belief, fantasy, and invention."[11]

The drive within Anselm to win the faith of others is an external manifestation of the need to believe in himself. For that reason, the lies that he tells and the deceptions that he perpetrates sharply impact his own view of reality. When he fakes suicide in order to convince Maria of his love for her, the other characters see through the charade almost at once. Yet Anselm does not give up the pretense immediately, because he has almost convinced himself that he is dead. Regine interprets the situation correctly when she says that it is possible for him to talk himself into a thing so completely that he is willing to let himself suffer for it.

Anselm's ultimate exposure by the detective Stader is more than simply revelation of his lying and philandering. It is a total destruction of the world created by Anselm's sense of possibility, a world that has been so much a part of the lives of the others that its collapse signals a violent shattering of their illusions as well. Once that framework has broken down, Anselm has no choice left but to return to mundane reality.

Unlike the other enthusiasts, Maria does not possess a sense of possibility that moves her to act on the basis of purely mental processes, either strongly rational (Thomas), creative-fantasizing (Regine), or a combination of the two (Anselm). Rather, her search for truth is based completely upon emotional response.

Maria's perception of life is totally subjective. Accordingly, her sense of possibility responds to people and things that call up from within her specific feelings—of worth, of being needed, of faith in something outside herself. Anselm describes her approach to finding what she desires, when he says that she sees him as a romantic hero and expects him to court her in medieval fashion. In that sense, she "corresponds in large measure to the classical concept of the 'noble lady,' " who is characterized by moderation and dignity, while remaining passive in love, allowing herself to be courted rather than playing the seductress.[12]

Despite the revelations about Anselm's true nature, he has succeeded in stimulating Maria's desire to feel and believe. He has thus given her something that she does not have within the framework of her marriage to Thomas. That explains why, when Anselm leaves the house, she follows him, even though she knows that he is a phony. Speaking to Thomas, she justifies her action by saying that happiness depends upon things that cannot be calculated or predicted, things that are simply there, even though they may not be right. She sees Anselm as having given her something of that kind.

Viewed as a whole, *The Enthusiasts* is an illustration of possibilities for approaching life. At the end of the play the alternatives remain open. Musil gives no answer to the question of who is right, because in his eyes there is no final, definitive answer, only possibilities from which the audience, like his characters, may choose at will.

In his only other creation for the stage, *Vinzenz and the Girl Friend of Important Men*, Musil introduced the main themes and many of the subordinate motifs from *The Enthusiasts* into a new framework of satire and irony. The special relationship between the two dramas has caused critics to characterize the farce about the swindler Vinzenz as the "satyr play" to the earlier, more serious production.[13]

From Musil's avowed perspective of taking neither the world nor the theater seriously in writing it, *Vinzenz and the Girl Friend of Important Men* offers humorous commentary on the issues that are the center of attention in *The Enthusiasts*. Among the devices that the author employed to achieve his comic effect are a clearly defined modern chorus of "satyrs" in the group of "important men" who court the heroine Alpha, and a figure who corresponds to the classical chorus master Silenus. Like Silenus, Halm, Alpha's husband, often functions as a commentator and choreographer of the "satyrs' " actions and as an intermediary between the "important men" and the major protagonists.

The satyr play of antiquity often had implications broader than its specific relationship to the tragedies with which it was directly associated. In like manner, Musil's comedy parodies not only *The Enthusiasts* but also other dramatic works of the time. It is clear that *Vinzenz and the Girl Friend of Important Men* deliberately satirizes the type of theater of which the creations of such popular dramatists as Frank Wedekind, Georg Kaiser, and Carl Sternheim are representative. Alfred Kerr, in his first review of the play, described it as "an often funny parody of the expressionistic pieces that have been written in the manner of Wedekind,"[14] while Günther Schneider emphasized specifically the parallels between Musil's work and Wedekind's comedy *The Marquis von Keith*.[15]

Overemphasis of the connections between *Vinzenz and the Girl Friend of Important Men* and expressionist drama, however, led Musil's contemporaries to misunderstand his artistic intentions. In a letter to his friend Franz Blei, Musil complained that reviewers, almost to the man, had misinterpreted his work by associating it with the productions of Wedekind and others. To the extent that such interpretations failed to place the farce within the context of his oeuvre as a whole, his complaint was justified.

By his own admission, Musil wrote *Vinzenz and the Girl Friend of Important Men* for the specific purpose of opening his way to the stage. His particular concern was to break down the barriers that prevented *The Enthusiasts* from taking its rightful place in the theater repertoire. He hoped that a work that offered major ideas from the first play in a less tedious, more palatable form would serve as a bridge to critical and public understanding of what he considered to be his dramatic masterpiece.

Among the pertinent elements from *The Enthusiasts* that are presented in new variation in *Vinzenz and the Girl Friend of Important Men* are the treatment of life as a continual choosing from among alternatives, the search for identity in reunion with the childhood self, escape into the "Other Condition" through the creative exercise of fantasy, and the definition of the main protagonists as "enthusiasts" who are more at home in the realm of ideas than in reality.

Through renewed use of more specific features, the exploration of these general themes from a different perspective is linked even more carefully to their treatment in *The Enthusiasts*. Included among these telltale characteristics are the problem of pointed conflict between ideas and human behavior, the prominent figure of the swindler as a player of roles, the motif of the fantastic lie, and the staging of a fake suicide. All of these components are woven together in a fabric of satire that is neither sarcastic nor derisive, neither cynical nor brutal, but rather playfully ironic in its exposure of the shallowness of middle-class existence.

In contrast to *The Enthusiasts* and Musil's early prose creations, *Vinzenz and the Girl Friend of Important Men* has a relatively well developed plot. The story line focuses initially on Alpha, a femme fatale who has drawn to herself a circle of "important men," stereotyped representatives of modern capitalistic civilization. Alpha toys with her admirers, leaving them hanging between intimacy and rejection. At the beginning of the play, the relationship has reached a point of crisis. The rich merchant Bärli has grown weary of being humiliated, and he attempts to force Alpha to abandon her perpetual playing with possibilities and to make a decision. Tying her up, he points a pistol at her and threatens to kill both her and himself unless she promises to marry him.

The tension of the scene is broken when Vinzenz responds to Alpha's cries for help by emerging from his hiding place behind a chair. He explains his presence by saying that he wants to continue a conversation with Alpha that they had left unfinished ten years earlier. Before he can pursue his stated objective, the trio is joined by Alpha's impotent husband, Dr. Apulejus-Halm, who has come by invitation to celebrate Alpha's name day. Halm views himself as Alpha's "creator" and serves as a kind of cicerone to the admirers who soon arrive to join in the celebration. Meanwhile, Alpha retires to her room to rest, and Bärli withdraws to write his letters of farewell.

In the second act Vinzenz takes up the desired conversation with Alpha. After reflecting on their youthful love affair, they discuss Vinzenz's plan to use an infallible system and working capital provided by the "important men" to break the banks of the world's casinos and thereby become rich and powerful. Their dialogue is interrupted by Bärli, who comes in waving his pistol, fires it at Alpha and then himself, and falls to the floor. The shots, however, are blanks. Bärli soon gets up again and reveals that the whole scene has been staged by Vinzenz in an effort to cure the merchant of his trivial infatuation with Alpha. Although Alpha's friends accept the proposal that they become "stockholders" in Vinzenz's money-making scheme, the scam collapses when Vinzenz is exposed as a swindler.

During the final act, the "important men" try to restore the harmony that Vinzenz has upset. They decide to entrust Alpha once more to the care of Halm, whom they view as an ally rather than a competitor. Alpha is then given an ultimatum; she must choose between the "important men" and Vinzenz. When her hope that Vinzenz will declare his love for her goes unrealized, rather than submit to the demands of her entourage of one-dimensional puppets, she accepts by telephone a previously rejected proposal of marriage. Vinzenz makes an unexpected decision of his own. He decides to become a servant.

The factor that links the main protagonists and central issues

of *Vinzenz and the Girl Friend of Important Men* most concretely
to the corresponding elements in *The Enthusiasts* is that of the
respective treatments of Musil's sense-of-possibility concept. Like
the four friends in the earlier play, Alpha and Vinzenz "are enthusiasts in Musil's sense, people for whom there is no attraction
in living 'really.' "[16] In that light, everything that they do contrasts
vividly with the rigidly fixed emptiness of the nameless "important
men," the scholar, the musician, the politician, the reformer,
and the young man, who collectively symbolize the stagnation
of a society in which ideas are a threat to the status quo rather
than a stimulus for change. Alpha characterizes Vinzenz and
herself succinctly but accurately when she says that he is someone
whom nothing can bind, just as she is.

In the figure of Vinzenz the sense of possibility manifests
itself most directly as creative fantasy. He employs this faculty
on several levels to shape his own life and manipulate the lives
of others. Like Anselm in *The Enthusiasts*, he exploits the situations that he encounters by playing roles appropriate to his
purposes. Vinzenz is a clever confidence man and "fantastic liar"
who has little difficulty in pointing his victims in the desired direction. In addition to acting out selected parts himself, he also
creates roles for others whom he moves to play the scenes that
he devises. Employing this capability in another variation, he
also has the capacity to transform reality into theater.

When selecting his roles, Vinzenz is careful to distinguish
between parts that allow him to maintain his freedom, and the
constraining, yet hollow personae of middle-class reality. For example, his sense of possibility permits him to envision himself
in the position of an individual with the power and money to do
as he pleases. He says at one point that to want to be Caesar or
Goethe or Lao-tse is a banality. Then he goes on to suggest that
the situation changes if one really is such a person. Specifically,
money will give him the potential to be anything that he wants
in politics, art, moral philosophy, or any of life's other affairs,
while at the same time permitting him to destroy what he does
not like. On the other hand, he could play the roles represented

by Alpha's admirers only if he were somehow flawed. At one point he mockingly laments the fact that he has not even the smallest defect. A blemish of some sort would cast him in a role corresponding to those of Alpha's "important men," but he is unfit for such a part because he is "incurably sound." His ability to reject what is serious in life gives him a vitality and humanness that the "important men" do not possess.

Vinzenz's most impressive demonstrations of the creative strength of his sense of possibility occur in his manipulation of others. Two scenes in which he emerges as the director of "theatrical performances" offer vivid illustrations of this point. The first is the situation in which he persuades Bärli to perform the cathartic fake murder-suicide routine. By persuading the merchant that acting out his passion will set him free of Alpha, Vinzenz uses the power of suggestion to change possibility into reality.

In the second instance, the transformation occurs in the reverse direction. As the "important men" and Alpha's bisexual girl friend attempt to win Alpha back to the relationship that existed before Vinzenz's arrival, the girl friend reveals that she has had an affair with Vinzenz. This confession leads to blows between the two women, and Alpha suddenly appears in a bad light before her companions. Vinzenz saves her from embarrassment by claiming that Alpha's angry response was staged as a demonstration of her acting talent. The following lines show how Vinzenz's creative instinct enables him to seize complete control of the situation by reshaping reality as theater:

All *unbelieving:* That was an act?
VINZENZ: But of course. *He helps* ALPHA *up. Then to the girl friend:* You'll have to forgive us. For the sake of naturalness we couldn't tell you. *To all:* There is nothing, as you know, for which Alpha would not have extraordinary talent, but a sample was required. It was insisted that she turn the next best trivial provocation into a "scene." For we only use scenes that arise out of life itself; only they are completely natural.

At the end of the play, when Vinzenz makes his decision to

become a servant, Alpha suggests that she could do the same thing and that they could then work together. Vinzenz rejects her proposal, saying that he would ask her to go somewhere else because they are perhaps too much alike after all. By emphasizing the similarities between them, he underscores the fact that they are tied together by the shared sense of possibility that places them both at odds with the mundane world of reality.

Like Vinzenz, Alpha consciously uses her vision of life's alternatives to manipulate her surroundings. According to Bärli, she twists life so that everything looks different and new. In a conversation with her girl friend, Alpha vividly demonstrates her awareness of the creative power that she possesses in contrast to the representatives of the stagnant bourgeois society. Pointing to the girl friend's inability to think ambiguously, she emphasizes her own capacity to change a color from black to white, or a funeral dress into a wedding gown, simply by willing her perception of them to be so. It is this very ability to see things in another light that gives her control over the "important men."

In contrast to her rigidly defined admirers, Alpha is the embodiment of ambiguity, ceaseless change, endless possibility. Egon Naganowski has accurately characterized her unfixed nature by describing her as a mixture of capriciousness, vanity, selfless impulses, ruthless mischief, cunning, ingenuousness, seductive coquetry, destructive coolness, fierce aggressiveness, and all-encompassing indifference.[17]

Because they do not share this intrinsic mutability with her, Alpha rejects both the "important men" and their world. In describing to Vinzenz her past life as a continual process of considering possibilities, she insists that he must not despise her because of the people that he has seen with her. After all, she has, of course, tried things from different angles, but she has never taken them seriously.

The barrier that she places between herself and her admirers is a denial that they are human. It takes the form of a constant hammering at their fixed natures. Specifically, she stresses their lack of contact with the other possibilities that lie beyond a narrow purview. In response to her husband's assertion that she controls her gentlemen friends by reproaching them for not being something else, Vinzenz finally understands that by chiding the intellectual because he is not a businessman, the musician because he is not a scholar, and the businessman because he is not a musician, Alpha communicates to each of them that they are not human. As a result each suddenly notices that his life is foolish.

Alpha's strongest expression of a claim to the right to continue living outside the stultifying restrictions of her suitors' ordered existence, is given in the label that she applies to herself. In a vehement outburst to Vinzenz, she asks him at one point if he knows what an anarchist is. She then insists that she is an anarchist and that she will remain one for as long as she lives. In so saying, she establishes firmly her identity as an enemy of order and an explorer of the infinite realm of possibility.

Musil's original title for his first play was not *The Enthusiasts* but rather *The Anarchists*. That fact suggests an intent to demonstrate that people who have a well-developed sense of possibility are outsiders with respect to modern social order. By her own words, Alpha declares herself to be such an outsider. Like the four friends in *The Enthusiasts*, she must find within herself the answer to the question of the right life. Just as the characters in the earlier play give only possibilities from which to choose, so Alpha "tells nobody what sort of a person one should be, for she embodies eternal questions without answers."[18]

5

~~~~~~~~~~~~~~~~~~~~~~~~~~~~~~~~~~~~~~~

Man in Two Forms:
Three Women

The problem most central to Musil's lifelong literary preoccupation with the search for man's elusive identity, is that of the complementary relationship between the male and the female elements of the human condition. Artistically speaking, his clearest, most successful presentations of ideas pertaining to the mystery of the spiritual, even mystical, interdependency of the sexes are found in the novellas of *Three Women*.

The strength of this small volume and its importance within the context of modern German literature are reflected in the enthusiastic reception that it enjoyed during Musil's lifetime, and in its continuing popularity as the best known of his books. A measure of this particular work's lasting impact is suggested in the comments of one of Musil's admirers, who wrote to him in 1930: "There are more eloquent books of world literature, that are more passionately exciting than the *Three Women*, but there is none with the sharpness and illuminating power, with the long-forgotten beauty of this small book."[1]

Although the three stories are extremely different from each other in setting, mood, tone, and plot, they share major themes, perspectives, and approaches to the man-woman focus of narrative tension. Each of the tales features a man whose confrontation with a previously unknown side of himself is mediated by a woman who symbolizes a foreign, irrational dimension of existence. All of the accounts are presented from the masculine perspective, and each of them offers a different variation of the unfaithfulness theme that Musil explored from the feminine perspective in *Unions*.

In the new creations, the women figures represent for the men a special kind of gateway to the "Other Condition," and accordingly to a deeper understanding of the self. Musil later carried this notion to its symbolic extreme in *The Man without Qualities*, where the characters Ulrich and Agathe are metaphorically juxtaposed as alternative versions or complementary halves of a single individual.

Within the novellas of *Three Women*, the title figures force the respective men to make decisions concerning the acceptance of newly revealed aspects of their identities as human beings. In each instance the male character is torn away from normal relationships, with the result that his established pattern of life is threatened. The manner in which he deals with the crisis that arises out of his connection to the woman forms the primary substance of the story.

The result may be either constructive or destructive. If the man cannot cope in the real world with the implications of what he has learned about himself, he must destroy either himself or the generator of the revelation, the woman. The first option is illustrated in *Grigia*, the second in *Tonka*. If, on the other hand, he is strong enough to face the new reality, he has the opportunity to forge himself into a being who is in dynamic harmony with the feminine component of his life, as does the hero of *The Lady from Portugal*.

In many respects the first novella of the collection, *Grigia*, is a kind of masculine version of *The Perfecting of a Love*. Elements common to both stories include the initial separation of a husband and wife who enjoy a positive marital relationship, removal of one member of the pair into an isolated place apart from normal reality, manifestation of a longing for reunion with the beloved on a mystical rather than physical plane, and entry into an adulterous union that somehow facilitates the desired per-

fect rejoining of the separated marriage partners. There is a significant difference, however, in the intensity of the respective
experiences. In *Grigia*, the union that occurs in the spiritual realm
renders its seeker unable to survive any longer in the real world.

The external events that form the novella's plot are not at
all complex. Homo, a geologist and private consultant, declines
to join his wife and sick child in a prolonged stay at a sanitorium.
He accepts an invitation to join an expedition to reopen some
Venetian gold mines in a remote area of northern Italy. As the
work moves forward, he loses himself in the new environment
and breaks off contact with his distant wife. In response to the
warm reception that he has received in the valley, he begins an
affair with the peasant woman Lene Maria Lenzi, whom he calls
"Grigia," the gray one, after her cow of the same name. When
Grigia eventually attempts to terminate the relationship, he pre-
vails upon her to join him in one last intimate encounter. While
they are together in an abandoned tunnel, Grigia's husband seals
off the entrance with a large stone. Somehow Grigia escapes
through a crevice, but Homo has neither the strength nor the
will to follow her back into the outside world.

Virtually all of the story's narrative power derives from the
tension between the two competing male-female relationships in
which Homo is involved. The interplay between his affair with
Grigia and the spiritual implications of his marriage represents
the conflict between the real-physical and the ideal-mystical sides
of his nature. In the process of the struggle, Homo subordinates
his old, real-world-oriented persona to the newly revealed spiritual
aspect of his being, rather than striving to establish a harmony
between the two. When he uses Grigia as a vehicle for his "ride"
into the mystical dimension, she abandons him there, closing
the gate to his return.

Like Musil's earlier prose creations, *Grigia* begins as a quest
for at-oneness with the self. Homo refuses to join his family on
the trip that is necessary for his son's cure, because it seems to
him that it would separate him from himself and everything that

means anything in his life for too long a period of time. The resulting physical separation, however—this symbol for a love that has become somehow divisible because of the child—does not immediately lead to the expected internal unity, but rather to "a sort of self-dissolution" that the narrator equates directly with the parting of man and wife. Accordingly, from that point on, Homo's adventure becomes the search for reunion with a lost part of himself, a spiritual dimension that is embodied in his now-distant mate.

Within the isolated world of his geological expedition, Homo intensifies the sense of physical detachment from his wife by breaking off his correspondence with her. At the same time, he tries to enter into harmony with the natural environment on a spiritual-mystical level. That is, he attempts to transcend the limitations of reality and expand his consciousness of his own being by penetrating into the "Other Condition." The result is a powerful revelation concerning his relationship to his wife and the true meaning of their separation. In the context of this visionary experience, his self-image and his conception of his wife begin to merge.

The scene that describes this critical turning point begins with his attainment of an understanding of the implications of isolating himself from his family for the summer. Alone in the woods, he sinks to one knee and spreads his arms. The movement seems to become a self-embrace that lifts him spiritually away from his body. He seems to feel his wife's hand, hear her voice, and respond accordingly, with the result that he undergoes a personal inner transformation. There is a sudden intensification of his feeling of both physical and spiritual dependency upon his wife. He recognizes that his inner being is connected as much to her body as to his own, and that their respective experiences of basic human sensations and needs, such as hunger, weariness, hearing, and seeing, are inseparably intertwined.

The vision culminates in Homo's release from the bonds of reality, and in his achieving reunion with his soul, the feminine aspect that is symbolized in his mind by his wife. Significantly, that realization of his desire is accomplished by a spiritual return to the world of youth, the sphere that Musil's "enthusiasts" and other characters attempt in vain to reenter. Although he is not a religious man, he experiences a moment of inner illumination. His thoughts become lost in a bright burst of emotion, and he is impressed with the realization that all of the aspects of his quest find a culminating focus in the concept of reunion.

The impact of the event upon him is profound. It frees him of both his desire to live in the physical world and his fear of death, and prepares him for what ultimately takes place during his final meeting with Grigia in the tunnel. From the day of his illumination on, Homo is simply looking for a place and an opportunity to die.

Grigia's role in what happens to Homo is more complex than the simple participation in an adulterous liaison. On one level, she serves as a proxy for his wife in physically reinforcing the new union with the female half of his being. Since the wife of his ideal projection is his fantasy representation of the absolute feminine principle, Grigia can become a substitute for her in the process of Homo's final journey toward the fulfillment that he will find in escape from reality. In this respect she illustrates Musil's concept of the interchangeability of individuals as symbols, an idea that is given special emphasis near the beginning of the story through its direct introduction in another context.

Homo himself becomes fascinated with the possibility of one person stepping into the identity of another when he hears the account of an incident in which a stranger moved around the area and persuaded one woman after another that he was her long-lost husband, newly returned from America. The replacements succeeded because the women were willing, even eager to accept his story, and because there was no conflicting claim strong enough to prevent them from doing so. The real husbands were too far away to act in their own behalf. For Homo, the fact that such an exchange could occur here strongly influences his perception of the region and its people, especially the women, and contributes to the detached, almost-impersonal manner in which he quickly enters the affair with Grigia.

On a second level, the peasant woman is a symbol in her own right of the feminine aspect of Homo's nature. In this connection, Frederick G. Peters relates her to C. G. Jung's definition of the anima as "the unconscious and latent feminine side of the male that complements his conscious masculinity."[2] Peters's discussion of the parallels between Musil's story and Jung's ideas focuses especially on the notion of the anima as a seductress who is typically associated with a variety of animal symbols.[3] Jung's theories, however, were unfamiliar to Musil. It is therefore important to note that within the context of his works as a whole, animal metaphors and images are used in a much broader sense to represent simply the aspect of individual identity that is missing, regardless of the sex of the character concerned. For Homo, the animal symbols pertain to the feminine element, but for Veronica in *The Temptation of Quiet Veronica* they are clearly related to the masculine dimension.

In a clearer fashion, Homo's mistress represents the physical, animal world that he must eventually forsake in order to progress into the higher realm where the spiritual union with his other self can become permanent. Homo consciously associates the woman with the lower order of existence when he gives her the nickname "Grigia."

As the narrative continues, she and the other inhabitants of the village are connected with animal imagery that emphasizes Homo's increasing psychological removal from his former reality. Breakdown in communication is especially symptomatic of the withdrawal from normal relationships that is catalyzed by his exposure to the rural environment. When the participants in the excavation venture gather socially in the parsonage courtyard twice a week, their conversation degenerates to primitive interchange that is hardly language at all. They are described as communicating in something akin to sign language, which, although it employs words, is really nothing more than the language of animals. At the same time, the situation when Homo is with Grigia has the simplicity and magic that Homo associates with an early experience in the village, which involved horses, cows, and a dead pig. Significantly, the most important aspect of this animalistic enchantment is the problem that Homo and Grigia have in communicating, a difficulty that arises specifically out of the fact that Grigia uses "a magical language."

The most vivid reduction of Grigia to animal symbols occurs in the final scene of the story, when she reacts to her husband's sealing of the entrance to the tunnel. In this instance she is depicted as kneeling by the barrier, pleading and angry, swearing that she is innocent of wrongdoing, and that she will remain so. In the final pertinent sentence of the description, the narrator equates her actions with those of a squealing pig and a maddened horse. From the perspective of this portrayal, her return to the outside world is in harmony with the notion that her faithfulness to the external, physical reality enables her to go on living there. By the same token, Homo's inability or unwillingness to follow her signals his final break with the lower, animal order of existence.

Helmut Gumtau has interpreted *Grigia* as a parable illustrating the idea that "adultery is destruction of the ego."[4] Such a reading fails to take into account the sequence of events in the story. Just as Claudine, in *The Perfecting of a Love*, achieves her goal in a mystical experience that occurs prior to her physical submission to the official, so the illumination that prepares the way for Homo's death takes place in isolation, before he ever meets Grigia. For both Claudine and Homo, the act of adultery is nothing more than a secondary, outward performance. It confirms and seals an inner change that has already happened, determining the future for each of them.

Like *Grigia*, the second novella of the collection, *The Lady from Portugal*, presents the problem of tension between the masculine and feminine dimensions of the hero's existence as a matter that threatens to destroy him, unless a viable balance between them can be achieved. Aside from the external details of setting and plot, the major difference between the two stories is that Ketten, the Portuguese lady's husband, develops the inner strength that is necessary to achieve such an equilibrium within the real world, while Homo does not. In that respect, Ketten is unique among Musil's characters. No other major figure in the novels, plays, or novellas attains a state of *lasting* harmony between the male and female, the real and ideal, the rational and irrational aspects of his or her being. This rare accomplishment forms the focus for what Frederick G. Peters has called "artistically the most perfect of all of Musil's fiction."[5]

As a work of art, *The Lady from Portugal* is the most traditional and most colorful of Musil's creations. Its structure and development resemble those of a classical fairy tale. Vivid and detailed descriptions of landscape contribute a richness of narrative fabric that is seldom visible elsewhere in the author's writings. The specific symbols that give the work much of its meaning and direction are clear and powerful, and the story's substance does not disappear behind the extended essayistic patterns that so often render Musil's prose dense and even opaque. Helmut Gumtau accurately characterizes the novella's literary strength when he describes it as the high point of Musil's novella art, a balladlike, yet realistic story that is written in a solid, concise style in realization of the author's goal to perfect the laconic definite element and the richness of that which is incidental.[6]

Unlike all of Musil's other major creations, *The Lady from Portugal* is cast in a setting that is clearly removed from the modern world. The time is the Middle Ages, the place, a somewhat indefinite wild and isolated locale near the Brenner Pass on the border between Austria and Italy. Within this temporal and physical frame, real and unreal happenings merge and interweave with one another to the point that they become almost indistinguishable.

The pertinent external events are these: Ketten, a member

of an old line of feudal barons, uses the traditional courtship year in the South to win as his bride a beautiful young Portuguese woman. After bringing her home to his lonely estate, he carries on a fight against his enemy, the Bishop of Trent. The struggle lasts for eleven years, until the bishop finally dies. During this time, Ketten seldom comes home, and then only briefly, and his wife and children remain strangers to him. When the bishop's death sends Ketten back to his wife at last, a crisis occurs. During the homeward ride, he is bitten by a fly, with the result that he becomes mortally ill. After a doctor ministers to him, he has himself carried to his estate. By an act of will he seems to resist the further progress of the disease, but he does not begin to recover. A childhood friend of his wife comes to visit, and Ketten perceives him as an intruder against whom he is helpless. Nothing changes until a small cat appears. The kitten seems to take upon itself Ketten's illness. Ketten, his wife and her friend watch it grow sick, and they sense that it represents their individual destinies. With the death of the animal comes Ketten's partial regeneration, but he still remains unable to reclaim his former health and strength. Finally he challenges himself to perform a feat that will end the uncertainty of his future and determine whether he is to live or die. Exerting himself in a tremendous effort, he scales the sheer cliff below his fortress. When he then goes to his wife's bedchamber to confront the friend whom he suspects of intruding on his marital rights, he finds his wife alone. Her countryman has already left the castle.

Ketten's course toward the balanced and harmonious existence that he achieves at the end of the novella is a process of self-definition. It takes the form of an agonizing rebirth in which he must either establish his true identity or die.

He begins his quest from a state of uncertainty and ambiguity in which everything that might characterize him as an individual remains hovering between possibilities. His home locale is situated indefinitely between north and south, and his origins are neither purely German nor Italian. He follows the pattern of his forebears

who sided at times with the Guelphs, at times with the Ghibel-
lines, whichever seemed in their best interest, but never felt that
they owed allegiance to anyone or anything other than themselves.
During the year of his courtship, in the feminine realm of his
prospective bride, he reveals himself as a perfect gentleman, while
in the masculine domain of his ongoing warfare he is a rough
and hardened soldier. Yet even he does not know which pattern
of behavior, if either of them, reflects his real self.

From the beginning of the account it is evident that Ketten's
marriage to the Portuguese lady must ultimately provide the context in which the resolution of his search for identity will occur.
That fact is made very clear in the description of his life during
the years that he remains away from his wife. The period of his
struggle with the Bishop of Trent is specifically a time when his
true nature is "something that he might ride towards for many
weeks without reaching it." Only the infrequency and brevity of
his visits home, however, prevent him from discovering there
what he really is. According to the narrator, any lengthy stay
would have forced him to act in a manner consistent with his
actual essence. His characteristic absence from home thus becomes an external symbol for a continued shying away from self-
definition.

In that context the death of the Bishop of Trent terminates
the circumstances that have enabled Ketten to avoid the prolonged
exposure to the feminine realm of his wife, where the encounter
with self is inevitable. With the feud ended, he can no longer
hide behind a façade that makes him indistinguishable from his
ancestors. To survive, he must come forth as a new and independent individual.

Typically, Musil's protagonists progress to self-understanding
through their encounters with the "Other Condition." How they
cope with it depends on and therefore reflects what they are. In
the case of Ketten, the key that unlocks the gate to the "Other
Condition" is the sting of a fly; the doorway through which he
must pass is the ensuing illness. Heinz-Peter Pütz suggests that

the suffering caused by the sickness is itself Ketten's experience of the "Other Condition."[7] Only indirectly, however, does his disease mediate such an encounter by forcing him to spend a long period of time within his wife's sphere of influence. As the narrator indicates in the description of their initial journey to Ketten's estate, it is the mysterious Portuguese lady who continually lures her husband "on into some other realm." Under her ministrations, Ketten's soldier persona will be stripped away to reveal what lies beneath it.

Ketten's rebirth is more than simply survival of the mortal illness caused by the fly's bite. It is the result of specific decisions between possibilities. The regeneration itself occurs in stages that correspond to the definite exercise of the protagonist's volition. His first decision deals with his future at a very basic level. He must choose between life and death. Unlike Homo, Ketten still has the strength to resist the lure of death, but the struggle is not easy. Finally the day arrives when he realizes that death is imminent unless he can summon enough willpower to continue living. This realization is the turning point, and that night the fever subsides.

The resolve to remain alive is not sufficient in itself to bring about the change that will permit Ketten to emerge as a new being who can exist in harmony with his altered circumstances. It serves only to halt the progress of the disease, without providing the means to regain the health and strength that he needs in order to defend his right to life. Until he justifies his continued existence through an additional act of will, he remains vulnerable.

What is required of Ketten is a peculiar rite of passage. A fortune-teller gives him a general indication of what he must do, but leaves him to discover the specifics for himself. She says only that he will be cured when he accomplishes a task.

His subsequent course leads him in the same direction that other Musil figures have taken in their respective efforts to escape current reality. He turns to the past, to the period of youth, when creative fantasy maximizes the sense of possibility. Unlike earlier characters, however, Ketten eventually recognizes that youth itself is not the final goal. Rather he must realize a youthful aspiration in order to transcend to something of far greater worth that lies beyond it. As he struggles with and rejects his old warrior life and the new experience of suffering as possible definitions of his future existence, the life-giving task becomes visible to him in the challenge to realize an insane dream that he had entertained during his childhood, the dream of scaling the sheer cliff below his ancestral castle. As he contemplates the possibility of doing it, the task assumes the proportions of a trial by ordeal or the performance of a miracle. This accomplishment of what appears to be an impossible feat is the ultimate test of the sense of possibility, a test by which Ketten may become in the fullest sense the man that he has the potential to be.

In presenting the process of Ketten's painful metamorphosis, Musil employs several animal symbols to accent important relationships. During his battle years, for example, the protagonist is cast repeatedly in the image of a wolf. His wife's ultimate mastery over that side of his being is foreshadowed early in their marriage, when she tames a young wolf and makes a pet of it. She is described as loving the wolf because its sinewiness, its brown pelt, and the quiet ferociousness and power of its gaze remind her of Ketten.

Later, as the illness forces Ketten to confront the possibilities for self-definition that may be open to him, he symbolically rejects his old persona by ordering a servant to kill the wolf in what Johannes Loebenstein has called "an act of the will to be free."[8] Ironically, what remains of the hero's earlier identity at that point is the being that the wild animal has become within the Portuguese lady's sphere of influence. When the narrator portrays Ketten in the feeble condition that characterizes him when his wife's friend arrives, he compares the sick man to a dog lying shame-filled in the grass.

The most powerful and complex animal symbol in all of Musil's literary works is the small cat that suddenly intrudes into the lives of the characters in *The Lady from Portugal*. The cat is a sign, initially incomprehensible to those who encounter it, that points the way for Ketten's redemption. By watching its peculiar "martyrdom," Ketten and his wife become observers of the transformation process from a perspective that eventually enables the protagonist to employ creatively the possibilities of the "Other Condition" in the realization of his own destiny.

In the illness of the kitten Ketten inescapably recognizes his own destiny. Specifically, the cat's dwindling away and eventual death symbolize the spiritual course that Ketten must follow, a course toward release from the restrictions of current reality. That is, even the last vestiges of his animal self—the weakened, helpless dog that remains after the wolf is dead—must be destroyed if Ketten's true human identity is to manifest itself. In pointed reflection of what the cat's sacrifice represents, the narrator describes it as "a metamorphosis into a human being." The cat thus becomes a symbol not only for the Ketten persona that must die, but also for its replacement. As the man contemplates climbing the cliff, he senses that what will emerge from that venture will be "not he but the little cat from the world beyond," or that more perfect self whose home is in the "Other Condition."

Where Grigia is primarily the reality-bound, passive vehicle of Homo's escape into what for him is a more desirable realm, the Portuguese lady is both an active facilitator of Ketten's final transformation and a rich symbol for the goal toward which he strives in his search for identity.

By the very act of moving into Ketten's world, a place that she finds "unimaginably hideous," his wife transforms the stark environment into something that is no longer compatible with the Ketten who lived there prior to her coming. In addition to her silent beauty, she contributes an air of mystery and magic that somehow give new and unfamiliar parameters to the happenings within the castle. Even Ketten's fellow soldiers sense that a change has taken place. For that reason, there grows up around him a new legend, that he has sold his soul to Satan, out of hatred for the bishop of Trent, and that the devil now inhabits his castle in the form of his beautiful foreign wife. When he finally returns home to combat the disease that threatens his life, he encounters a domain in which the famous doctor who is summoned to treat him can do nothing, and his fever subsides only after his wife has marked magical symbols on the door and the posts of his bed. Only through the care of his Portuguese lady is he placed in a position where he can consciously exercise his will to live and symbolically slay his former self in the figure of the pet wolf.

Ketten's wife plays an even more direct role in bringing him to the point where he is able to make the final step toward complete rebirth. When the cat's suffering has fulfilled its purpose in arousing within the couple the feeling that it has somehow taken upon itself Ketten's illness in order to enable him to live, it is the woman who orders the animal to be killed, thereby precipitating the events that follow.

As a symbol for the mystery of life that Ketten seeks to unravel, the Portuguese lady takes on almost classical dimensions. In a very real sense she corresponds to the eternal feminine principle that Johann Wolfgang Goethe identified at the end of *Faust* as the force that draws man toward his destiny. And like Goethe's Gretchen, who becomes Faust's guide in the afterlife, the Portuguese lady gives final meaning to what has happened to the man she loves. It is she who interprets most clearly the cat's role in Ketten's emergence as a renewed, harmonious being, when she equates its sacrifice with that of Christ in bringing to pass the resurrection from the dead. In the final lines of the novella she suggests that if God could become human, he could also take on the form of a cat. Although he realizes that his wife's words amount to blasphemy, Ketten does nothing to rebuke or contradict her, because both of them know that what she has said cannot escape from the confines of their private world in which it has its only meaning.

Unlike either *Grigia* or *The Lady from Portugal*, the last of the novellas in *Three Women* presents a situation in which the male protagonist ultimately rejects the feminine dimension as it is embodied in the title figure. He thereby maintains his established identity unchanged. In contrast to Homo, the unnamed young scientist in *Tonka* refuses to recognize the feminine mystical element as a valid determining factor for his future existence. He is also unprepared to enter a state of dynamic balance between the masculine and feminine aspects of life, as does Ketten.

Externally at least, the result is the exact opposite of what finally occurs in *Grigia*. The female figure dies, leaving her lover to maintain the position that he has defined for himself in the rational, material world. Her death, however, does not resemble Homo's act of self-liberation from reality. Rather, it is a painful martyrdom akin to the one endured by Ketten's kitten, an atonement of sorts for the sins of a modern, technological world in which faith no longer exists.

Of the stories in *Three Women*, *Tonka* was the most important for Musil and the most difficult for him to write. It documents in part his own intimate struggle with the feminine side of life. Although it is problematical in some instances to separate invented parts of the narrative from those with origins in Musil's specific experience, a number of situations and details are clearly autobiographical.

Interpreters of *Tonka* are quick to point to the parallels between the man-woman relationship that gives the tale its focus and Musil's early love affair with Herma Dietz.[9] His involvement with the simple working-class girl, beginning during his compulsory military year and continuing through the Stuttgart period and the time when he was working on his invention, corresponds in significant detail to the story of the lovers in the novella. Even the mother's opposition to her son's liaison with Tonka matches the continuing disagreement between Hermine Musil and Robert over the entanglement with Herma. It is unknown, however, whether or not the problem of Tonka's pregnancy and death is based on actual happenings.

The similarities between the respective family circumstances of the author and his protagonist are especially striking. Heinrich Reiter's role in Musil's parental home is duplicated in the figure of Uncle Hyacinth, a friend of the young man's parents who loves the mother and somehow fulfills needs that her husband cannot. Just as the boy Robert lived in tension with his home environment because he neither understood nor approved of the peculiar adult configuration, so the character in his story is shaped as to his attitudes by comparable conflicts. Like the author, the young engineer feels sorry for his father, quarrels with his mother and her friend, and resists the authority of the latter two individuals, openly rebelling against them.

Even more important is the depiction of the protagonist as a student of chemistry who refuses to consider any questions that cannot be dealt with on the basis of tangible, concrete reality. As such, he becomes what the narrator calls "a fanatical disciple of the cool, soberly fantastical, world-encompassing spirit of modern technology." This specific definition of the young scientist's nature connects his struggle directly to what Musil saw as his own early identification with the atmosphere of the times.

For all of that, the importance of *Tonka* within Musil's oeuvre lies not in its similarities to his own life. Rather, its value rests in its power as an artistic creation that illustrates from a new perspective ideas central to the author's work as a whole.

Although *Tonka* is presented in the third person, the psychological penetration of the male protagonist's mind is so intense and the perspective so clearly his that the account comes across almost like a first-person narrative. Musil's literary technique thus places the major emphasis not on the events of the story, but on the young man's response to them.

The plot is certainly not intricate. Tonka, an uncomplicated girl who works in a fabric shop, attracts the attention of the chemistry student, who recommends her for a position as companion to his ailing grandmother. Her simplicity, loyalty, and quiet nature draw him to her more and more, even though she remains a mystery to him. When the grandmother dies and Tonka prepares to return to live with her aunt, the scientist decides to take her with him to another city, where she becomes his mistress. After they have lived together for some years, Tonka becomes pregnant. Because the time of conception seems to correspond to a period when he was out of town, the protagonist refuses to believe that he is her child's father, even though she insists that she had no sexual relationship with anyone else. Nevertheless, he cannot bring himself to send her away, and they remain together during the pregnancy. As the birth of the baby nears, what appears to be a venereal disease manifests itself in Tonka. When the doctors find no evidence of disease in the scientist, he regards Tonka's illness as additional evidence of her infidelity. Both mother and child die shortly after Tonka gives birth, and the mystery remains unresolved.

Musil's failure to answer the question of how Tonka's child was conceived frustrates the superficial reader who is misled to believe that the mystery itself is the focus of the writer's concern. Christine Sjögren has however pointed out: "Because the author certainly does not deliver the deciding facts, we are forced to conclude that the problem of Tonka's conception, which has tormented scholars as well as her friend, cannot be answered at all and for that reason does not substantially determine the meaning of the novella."[10] Tonka's secret serves primarily as a point of departure for the presentation of an unpleasant parable about the viability of the one-sided individual who is characteristic of the modern world.

The specific effect of Tonka's pregnancy and illness upon her friend is to erect a barrier between the two lovers. It can be broken down only if he accepts the fact that other possibilities have weight at least equal to that of the conclusions he reaches based on "knowledge." Although he is willing to concede that other possible conclusions exist, he cannot bring himself to grant them any status of practical validity. He reasons that while such explanations for Tonka's condition are theoretically possible, they are really not probable. At the same time, he views the probability that he is not responsible either for her pregnancy or her illness as something close to surety.

As a committed representative of the twentieth-century technological order, the young scientist is a product of civilization's tendency to destroy or at least suppress the sense of possibility. The utter weakness of that faculty renders him completely unable, in his effort to penetrate to the truth of Tonka's being, to transcend the limits of empirical facts, logic, and rational argumentation. Because his perception of himself is unshakably rooted in fixed, material reality, any suggestion of circumstances that do not fit such a context threatens his very existence. It changes his identity, imbuing it with an uncertainty that is incompatible with his chosen life. Accordingly, to accept Tonka's claim that he is responsible for her condition has definite implications for his physical well-being. Despite the fact that the doctors have found no sign of Tonka's disease in him, the possibility of some unknown link between them frightens him. If he admits that she is right, then he himself becomes diseased.

By insisting that Tonka's version of the circumstances leading to her pregnancy is inconsistent with his world, the young scientist makes of her an intruder from a foreign domain to which he has no access. The nature of her native realm is reflected in her countenance and gives clues to her identity. As he looks at her face, Tonka's lover is confronted by impressions that seem to arise out of a world apart from the city's reality. He mentally associates her with cornfields, birds, the country air, and distance from the city, but also with a strange spiritual realm in which modern material concepts of "truth" do not exist. The only answer that makes any sense at all to him is that the young woman is living in the world of fairies, or of the sacred figures of religious legend.

Musil deliberately mingles the world of fairy tale with traditional religious images in the definition of Tonka's essence in the mind of her lover. In so doing, the author allies her to both creative fantasy and the mystical dimension that are complementary aspects of his ideal realm of infinite possibility. In each of the other novellas of the collection, that domain is equated with the feminine component of the hero's identity, an element of his life that initially remains out of reach. It is that part of him that exists in the "Other Condition" as the potential for completeness of being. In *Tonka*, the male protagonist's refusal to accept on faith what his mistress offers him as an alternative to familiar reality excludes him entirely from the prospects of expanding his own essence.

On a second level, the young man's unwillingness to grant that Tonka is what she professes to be places responsibility for her death directly upon him. The woman's destruction has several visible causes. Physically, she dies of the venereal disease that symbolizes her subjection to the infectious, devastating elements of modern civilization. Spiritually, she succumbs to her lover's lack of belief in her. From still another point of view it is her own vulnerability, her alienness, that makes her death inevitable. The metaphor that Musil uses to describe her fragility within the framework of influences playing upon her underscores her total nonviability in the practical, material world. He calls her "a snowflake falling all alone in the midst of a summer's day."

The death of Tonka as an individual and the question of how she became pregnant are not key issues for Musil. What *is* significant—and this is what the story is really all about—is the passing from modern life of what she symbolizes, and the failure of the basic relationship that is depicted in her rejected love for the young scientist. The narrator defines those two things when he says of Tonka: "She was Nature adjusting itself to Mind, not wanting to become Mind, but loving it and inscrutably attaching itself to it. She was like one of those animals that actually seek man's company."

Like Grigia, throughout the novella Tonka has difficulty in communicating with her lover. In his diary, Musil referred to her as one of the "poor girls who cannot speak." Within the present context that defines her as nature, the implications of the author's perception of his character are especially significant. In Tonka, nature has lost its power to speak and to be understood by the typical representative of twentieth-century society.

In that light, the young man's betrayal/rejection of Tonka identifies modern technological man as an entity alienated from its most basic origins and therefore its own fundamental essence. The story of the scientist and his mistress vividly illustrates that such a being has little hope of finding a way back to its lost soul, so long as the doorway to possibilities beyond empirical reality remains blocked by reason and material logic.

In a sense, Tonka's death without a final revelation of her secret offers the only positive note in the novella. By not giving the answer to that gnawing question concerning her apparent unfaithfulness, and by allowing her to remain true to herself, Musil preserves the realm of possibility, with its competing male and female dimensions, as the absolute state of man.

6

~~~~~~~~~~~~~~~~~~~~~~~~~~~~~~~~~~~~~~~

In Quest of Another Kind of Human Being: The Essays

The most significant product of Musil's continuing endeavor to define life's basic elements from the perspective of his own sense of possibility was the unshakable conviction that human existence can be different than it is. His belief in the potential for change colored the manner in which he looked at the world, its inhabitants, and his art. It shaped the characters and situations that he created in fiction and drama, but it determined even more vividly and concretely the direction and thrust of each of his many essays.

An integral relationship exists between Musil's narratives and plays on the one hand and his articles, critiques, and analytical and theoretical treatises on the other. He himself recognized that all of his writings had at least one common focus: the search for a new and different type of individual. While contemplating the publication of a collection of his essays, he considered various titles for the project. At one point, he proposed to call it *Attempts to Find Another Kind of Human Being*.[1] In an explanation of the title, contained in his diary, he wrote that it could actually stand as a valid heading for his complete works. Viewed in that light, in addition to offering pointed and critical analysis of the various phenomena in Musil's contemporary world, the essays give interesting information concerning his vision of the future.

At the center of Musil's essay concept are the development and exploration of ideas for their own sake. For him, "essay" means "attempt, but also possibility of thought."[2] The conjectural quality that he ascribed to these writings is reflected clearly in his private definition of the essay as a genre. In explaining what the cultivation of the essay meant to him, he emphasized his intention to give free play to his thoughts beyond the limit of what he could account for under all circumstances. The concept of speculation was an integral part of his perception of what an essay should be.

Taken as a whole, the nonfiction works thus form an important illustration of their author's reflective approach to the problems of his time. The essays reveal his powerful ability in the areas of abstraction and analysis, while presenting a personal history of ideas and thought processes pertaining to new ways of looking at humanity within the context of modern civilization.

What is perhaps most remarkable about the manner in which Musil conveys his ideas to the reader of these writings is the consistent artistry of his presentation. The material is not offered in cold statements of fact or even opinion, but through creative illumination of its different aspects. The critic Wilhelm Grenzmann has pinpointed some of the key factors in Musil's achievement of artistic effect. He writes: "Scientific objectivity is combined with accentuatedly subjective observation; there appears almost always in the essay the tendency toward artistic representation. The objectivity of the topic forces the author to devote himself to the subject, but the ego as a factor of judgment, evaluation, and representation moves the essay into the vicinity of the poetic work."[3]

An especially important contributor to the literary impression created by the essays is Musil's visible mastery of language. Although the author lamented the fact that his ideas often came across less effectively in the final versions of his articles than in prior forms of the same works, the published products reveal the rare facility with words that is one mark of the great poet. Helmut

Gumtau has accurately described the language of the essays and
reviews as extraordinarily diversified. He points specifically to the
simultaneous presence of laconic irony, lyrical imagery, contemplative accountings, and conversational tone as devices that the
author used to approach his object more closely through his
manner of expression.[4]

Although Musil's pamphlets, speeches, and contributions to
a variety of periodicals examine many contemporary problems in
substantial detail, they do not present a complete, organized philosophy of life. Rather, they are a replacement for an abstract
philosophical system, something that Musil regarded as unsuited
to the mediation of truth in a technological era, or to the exploration of concrete human issues. In the discarded plan to the
volume of essays that he was considering, he acknowledged concerning its potential contents their fragmentary nature and his
own inability to systematize them into a coherent philosophy.

Aside from their general focus then, the only real ordering
principle for Musil's essays is what they reveal about their author.
To that extent they are not unlike what the poet Johann Wolfgang
von Goethe considered his own writings to be: the fragments of
a grand confession. And like Goethe, Musil employed his technical and theoretical writings to involve himself in a broad spectrum of his era's intellectual concerns. Seen in that light, the
nonfiction studies that he produced become an especially personal
documentation of his continuing struggle with a problem that is
central to his works of literary art: the search for the right life.
The attempts to find a new kind of individual are thereby given
an added important dimension. They become acts in the quest
for an alternative self.

One significant aspect of the essays' revelation about Musil
is the degree to which they demonstrate how strongly his spirit
and ideas were informed by his Austrian origins. In her extensive
treatment of his nonfictional writings, Marie-Louise Roth characterizes the relationship between his attitudes toward modern
phenomena and his cultural heritage by stating that his opinions

about government, society, politics, literature, and art are informed by the spirit of the Austrian baroque period. Among the themes that she identifies as illustrative of the impact of this background upon his thoughts are: the connection between reality and idea, rejection of ceremonial form, the problematic relationship of the individual to social institutions, and the longing for order and leadership.[5]

Musil was well aware of his indebtedness to the Austrian cultural legacy, and that consciousness contributed to a certain dissatisfaction with himself as an essayist. The problem was that the tie to the past seemed to prevent him from realizing fully what he most deeply wished to accomplish: the creation of something new and different. Some of the frustration he felt in that regard is reflected in a diary entry about his reluctance to anthologize the journal articles. According to the passage in question, he rejected requests to publish an edition of the essays because he disliked their author as a man who did and wrote things that were not what he really wanted. This perceived lack of freedom was in part a result of the fact that most of the essays were commissioned rather than spontaneous productions. Yet it was also a reflection of the limitations imposed upon the writer by his own specific personality, the product of critical formative influences in his Austrian environment.

The topics of the essays are extremely diverse. Among them are war, internal Austrian and German politics, the nature of the state as a political entity, the problem of national and ethnic identities, the future of Europe, history, monarchy, revolution, aesthetics, morality, philosophical concepts, democracy, art, parliamentary government, ethics, and various social concerns. Musil illuminates individual writers, artists and works of art, as well as technical matters of science, engineering, law, medicine, and psychology. Articles on sports are mingled with discussions of pedagogy and creativity. In each instance, what matters is the ideas that are presented. There is never an offer of total resolution of a given problem, only a partial, tentative answer to the question:

What are the present and future possibilities for the individual produced by today's society?

Some general areas of concern receive more attention than others. One major domain that Musil explored rather extensively is that of ethics. In her examination of his theoretical writings, Marie-Louise Roth argues that ethical considerations are a primary focus of both the pre–World War I and postwar elucidations of contemporary problems. Specifically, she identifies the central focus of these essays as the question of preserving man's creative dimension by developing a technique that would permit scrutiny of life's relationships and consideration of its paradoxes while changing life itself so that the spirit continues to exist as an ethical-aesthetic force.[6]

Among the essays that illustrate most concretely Musil's ideas regarding the ethical dimension of human experience in different areas are "Das hilflose Europa oder Reise vom Hundertsten ins Tausendste" (Helpless Europe or journey from the hundredth into the thousandth), "Das Unanständige und Kranke in der Kunst" (The indecent and the sick in art), and "Skizze der Erkenntnis des Dichters" (Sketch of the understanding of the poet).

In "Helpless Europe or Journey from the Hundredth into the Thousandth," the author presents the demand for a new system of ethics in which an "overview of the reasons, the connections, the limitations, the fluid meanings pertaining to human motives and actions—an interpretation of life" must be presented in a convincing manner. The ethics that he requires would thus be in a position to revise completely the entire spiritual-cultural life of the society, in order to make social practices manageable and to be able to produce an "Other Condition" that is fundamentally different.

Similarly, matters of ethics and the need for a new, changed morality lie at the heart of Musil's argumentation in "The Indecent and the Sick in Art." The essayist is especially concerned with the inhibiting impact of traditional moral value systems upon artistic creativity. The direct stimulus for his comments is a visible frustration with public policy pertaining to continuing censorship. In polemicizing against restrictions that originate in external moral or ethical perceptions, he insists that art must be permitted to admit love even for things that are repulsive to human beings and in conflict with social order. His reasoning focuses on the idea that what is morally unacceptable in practical everyday life is transformed into something quite different within the context of a work of art. The final result of his examination of the problem is what Susan Erickson has called "a vision of moral evolution" that is based at least in part upon his interpretation of the writings of Friedrich Nietzsche.[7]

A critical factor in the development of the required new moral outlook is the contribution to be made by the writer. In "Sketch of the Understanding of the Poet," Musil defines the duty of the modern literary artist as the creation of fresh ethical possibilities. He says that the task is to discuss continually new solutions, relationships, constellations, and variables, to offer patterns for events and tempting models of humanity, and to invent the inner man.

According to Musil, the position of the poet in the contemporary world is determined by the fact that his domain is apart from that of man in the fixed rational sphere. To distinguish between the two opposing realms, Musil coined the terms "ratioïd" and "nonratioïd." The "ratioïd" province of practical reality is that of scientific system and organization of physical nature according to rules and laws. It is characterized by material facts, the dominance of repetition, and the ability of the facts to fit various groups of laws, rules, and concepts. By contrast, the "nonratioïd" dimension, "the home area of the poet," is the proper dwelling place of all that is unfixed, subjective, variable.

Musil's primary example of something that must be dealt with from the perspective of the "nonratioïd" is ethics, and more specifically morality. A change in approach to ethics is necessary because today's conceptions of morality are improperly and destructively bound to fixed principles. Musil views the prevailing ethic as methodically static because it is based upon inert concepts. For that reason, contemporary morality seems ready to collapse.

For Musil, the inadequacy of traditional ethics lies in the fact that morality is a matter of individual freedom and not of artificially imposed behavioral norms. The creative writer can contribute to the development of a more acceptable approach to ethical matters because in ethics, as in literary art: "The facts do not acquiesce . . . , the laws are sieves, happenings do not repeat themselves but are limitlessly variable and individual."

What is most important to Musil then, in his assessment of human ethical possibilities, is that they belong to the realm of ideas rather than absolutes. Because that is true, the poet as a promoter of ideas, whether they be ethical or aesthetic in nature, becomes more than simply a product of his times. The writer who is accomplishing his ordained task must become a "creator of the times."

Musil typically subordinates purely political concerns to the ethical, spiritual-intellectual, artistic, and social questions that are more important to him. Nevertheless, a significant number of his published articles offer analysis and criticism of the times from a distinctly political point of view. His commentaries on special Austrian problems such as the question of unification with Germany, conflicts among diverse ethnic populations, and Austria's role in the European community reveal a deep sensitivity to factors affecting the general political health of his native land.

What interests him most in this connection are the possibilities for the future that arise in a time of political transition, when the old order crumbles beneath the weight of inevitable progress in science, technology, and other fields that directly influence power configurations and the like. His essays reflect the notion that those prospects can only be realized most productively in the absence of formal government. In the early essay "Politisches Bekenntnis eines jungen Mannes" (Political confession of a young man) he described his stance as that of "a conservative anarchist." In most respects that characterization remained valid for his political position throughout his life.

Parallel to Musil's demand for a new ethic as a product of moral evolution is his insistence upon a new kind of state. Specifically, he envisioned a political evolution away from traditional patterns of government toward what he saw as a more natural form of human social organization. This point of view is illustrated very pointedly in the article "Der Anschluß an Deutschland" (The annexation of Austria to Germany). There he argues in favor of unification as a move in the preferred direction. Basing his position on factors of the adjacency of the two countries and the historical cultural relationship between them, he suggests that governmental unification is a decisive step away from what he labels "the state animal" and toward a truly human state. The only alternative is for Austria's "body" to go through a process of physical metamorphosis, something that would be far more difficult to accomplish than the projected union with Germany.

One of Musil's most interesting political essays is "Die Nation als Ideal und Wirklichkeit" (The nation as ideal and reality). This particular treatise, published in 1921, contains the "conservative anarchist's" response to what he perceived as the threat inherent in the steady growth of German nationalism. In it he explores the concepts of "nation," "race," and "state" as they relate to one another in the practical political context. Employing personally experienced history as background for his discussion, he develops arguments in support of the idea that a nationalistic focus for political action constitutes the misuse of an ideal. The problem lies in the mistaken equation of nation with either race or state, where state is the name given to governmental institution.

At the center of Musil's presentation is the notion that the essence of the nation as an ideal is a function not of ideology nor artificial community, but of the spirit of the individual. Concerning the attitude of the unhomogeneous populace toward the notion of a unifying group spirit, he insists that the designation of the German people as "We," where that appellation signifies a general commonality, does not represent reality. This view is illuminated in the contrasts between laborers and professors, profiteers and idealists, poets and movie directors. Musil argues that special interests make us into capitalists, proletarians, intellectuals, or Catholics, and accordingly dictate the real relationships between individuals. In that light, the concept of a national homogeneity becomes a blatant fiction. While he agrees then, for example, that races do exist, he insists that their character is determined by individuals. Therefore, any responsibility for determining what is good or bad rests with the individual and not the race. Otherwise ethics and morality will lose their value completely.

One important ramification of Musil's stance is that political and social responsibility is unavoidably placed as a burden upon the individual rather than upon governments or other composite groupings. In rejecting common tendencies to focus blame for the war and its results upon governments as represented by their functionaries, he insists that the excuse given by so many people— that they were not the guilty ones, but rather that the emperors, the generals, and the diplomats were—is false, because the people let the war happen without hindering it.

For Musil, the major flaw in the existing political establishment is that it fosters personal inactivity and powerlessness by limiting possibilities for response to problems that exist. He sees the prevailing relationship between individual and state as one of indulgence, and he suggests that indulgence per se describes the spirit of the times. As a result, no single person *can* act to change anything, and therefore nobody *does* act. To illustrate his point, he refers to the English and the Americans, who did not cause the children of central Europe to starve after the war, but who nevertheless allowed it to happen. He also indicts the Germans themselves, who may not have participated actively in perpetrating the horrors that occurred, but who were still guilty because of their passivity in letting things happen the way they did.

According to Musil, within this framework the only possibility for a single person to have an impact for change is through defiance of established rules and regulations. The exercise of freedom therefore becomes a matter of illegality, and the propagation of ideas is the province of heretics who challenge the state religion, writers who resist censorship, and other similar types who form the human counterweight to organization.

What Musil advocates as a replacement for the modern state is a more natural social order that fosters a true rather than a false ideal. Because he sees the concept of "nation" formulated in terms of race or government as a delusion in every form in which it has occurred, he believes that it must be replaced by an "unsystem" that promotes a human ideal of individual development based upon a reawakening of the facility for generating new ideas. In the resulting social evolution, the peoples who begin promptly to find their way from imperialism and nationalism to the new, possible world order will be the world's leaders and have the power to achieve their justified desires.

Ironically, Musil offers no guidelines for reaching his projected utopia. He suggests only that the possibility is there if the proper preparations are made. Even though it is not yet possible to define the path that will lead in the right direction, it is important to foster attitudes that will lead to the correct path.

To the extent that they contribute to the shaping of that desired attitude, Musil's essays on ethics, politics, social questions, and other matters complement the most important segment of his nonfiction writings, the articles, reviews, and theoretical studies pertaining to art, literature, and aesthetics. Representative works in this last group of essays focus on topics as specific as individual literary works and their authors, and as broad as the assessment of film's potentialities as a new art form, critical examination, and evaluation of literary movements such as expressionism, or questions concerning the nature of the poetic process and its creative possibilities.

Pertinent examples of his production in the area of literary criticism include the reviews "Bücher und Literatur" (Books and literature) and "Manas," and the article "Literarische Chronik" (Literary chronicle). Musil uses the occasion of his discussion of Paula Grogger's peasant novel *Das Grimmingtor (The Door in the Grimming)* in "Books and Literature" to come to grips with Austrian regional fiction. In his review of Alfred Döblin's book *Manas*, he expands his evaluation of a particular epic to include a more general treatment of the genre's role in modern literature. Exploring the nature of the epic per se, he presents his views on the function of myth and traces the replacement of the epic by the novel. "Literary Chronicle" is significant for what it reveals of Musil's perspectives on the creative possibilities suggested by the works of such writers as Franz Kafka, Robert Walser, Max Brod, and Arthur Hollitscher.

Among his best pieces of criticism are his evaluations of the theater. In addition to commenting on specific plays and performances, he often did in-depth studies of the performers and their careers. In the essay "Moissi," for example, written in 1921, he examined a prominent actor's performances in various roles, including those of Hamlet, Romeo, and Danton, among others. The journalist Oskar Fontana gave an accurate assessment of the quality of Musil's theater reviews when he stated that the author's critiques were among the most informative and unique ones that he had ever read. He especially emphasized the impartiality, the earnest point of view, and the intellectual framework of the essays as factors that made them special.[8]

No less meaningful for what they reveal of Musil's thought are the essays containing his theoretical statements about aesthetics. One of the most representative of these is "Ansätze zu neuer Ästhetik" (Rudiments of new aesthetics). Within the context of a presentation on the dramatic theory of film, with specific reference to a screenplay by the Hungarian writer Béla Balázs, Musil discusses his notion of the "Other Condition" as a second, mystical state of being, relating it directly to aesthetic experience. He clearly defines the "Other Condition" as the only alternative to the practical and fact-oriented normal state, suggesting that art is a powerful vehicle that enables man to transcend the limits of the real world. In describing the manner in which the experience of beauty functions as a catalyst for change within the individual, he emphasizes the observer's ability to compensate in other ways for imbalances of the conscious reality that are created by art. It is this capacity that enables the individual to restore to a new whole the self that has lost accustomed relationships, to convert the abnormal to a new norm, or to restore equilibrium to the disturbed soul.

Musil's view of artistic encounter as a doorway into the "Other Condition" parallels his approach to ethics and politics in the emphasis of individual perception over group values and judgments. The conservative political anarchist is also an artistic anarchist of sorts, who insists that works of art offer experience that is both direct and so individually unique as to be anarchic. It is this uniqueness of experience that separates the artistic creation from everything that has been said or done before and removes it from the realm of empirical knowledge into an entirely different dimension. To the extent that the "Other Condition" is the realm of the alternate inner self, art thus becomes a bridge to self-discovery, that, while anchored in normal physical reality, "arches away from the firm ground, as though it possessed an opposite abutment in the realm of imagination."

In the essay "Der Dichter und diese Zeit" (The poet and this time), Musil presented his strongest statement in support of the doctrine that true art and authentic artistic experience exist only as products of free, individual expression. The point of departure for his argument is his perception that the modern political tendency toward collectivism is a threat to the creative spirit, because it emphasizes community rather than individual interests. To illustrate his point, he suggests that in the realm of prose fiction, especially in the novel, individual destinies have been de-emphasized, with the result that "there is a certain partiality for sick, somewhat 'worm-eaten' 'heroes.'"

Musil views this trend as a parallel to the growing weakness in society that is manifested in the proliferation of formally organized human groups. The creation of new religious organizations and the like reflects a decline in self-reliance, the increased desire for leadership, and the growth of both external and internal dependency. Accordingly, it becomes the responsibility of the modern writer to restore human creativity on two levels. Internally, he must revive an art that is the product of individual genius, unrestricted by political or other external forces. Externally, he must use his art to uplift the individual within the society.

The important issue for Musil is the reclamation in literature of specific concepts that collectivist political tendencies have suppressed, concepts that are essential if the modern poet is to find his way to a new self-definition.

Musil openly laments the fact that contemporary political forces have made ideas like humanity, internationality, freedom, and objectivity unpopular by declaring them to be bourgeois, liberal, and old-fashioned. He views the gradual suppression of these concepts as a dangerous threat to the basic traditions upon which the poet so laboriously establishes his personal identity. In order to restore the writer to the position that he should occupy within the modern world, society must permit him to remain free of ideological restraints and even the demands of political exigencies. Anything else must inevitably lead to the degeneration of art, because what Musil calls the "aroma that is 'art' or 'geniality' " must remain "completely independent of place, time, nation, and race" if it is to survive.

Freedom from external restriction, whether political, ethical, or social, is necessary to the poet because without it the poet cannot accomplish the things that his spirit dictates. Most important, he cannot explore the new possibilities that are suggested in the freeing of ideas from old, fixed frameworks. To emphasize the absoluteness of his concept of artistic liberty, Musil claims for the poet the ability and the right to depict with the greatest degree of love things that he may privately abhor. Such a process would be the ultimate demonstration of the absolute freedom of the artistic spirit.

Musil concludes his plea for artistic freedom by expressing the hope that Europe may return to a conception of the artist that emphasizes the principle of individuality. In so doing, he cites as a spiritual precedent Wilhelm von Humboldt, to whom he attributes a definition of individuality as "a spiritual power that springs up without relationship to the course of events and begins a new series." In Humboldt's concept of creative genius Musil saw a possibility for producing both a different kind of art and the different kind of human being who would appreciate it.

7

Experimental Utopias: *The Man without Qualities*

All of Musil's other works, including *Young Törless*, the novellas, the plays, and the essays, can be interpreted as preliminary studies to his monumental unfinished novel *The Man without Qualities*. In each creation, the author tested variations of ideas about man's relationship to the world, his self-concept, and the possibilities for realizing greater fulfillment and more perfect humanity within the context of life's experience. The analysis of the human condition, with special reference to the role of the thinking individual in modern technological society, is the common denominator of his literary art and his theoretical writings. *The Man without Qualities* is the grand culminating experiment in his creative-analytic process of exploring the unfixed domain of mortal potentiality.

Musil's masterpiece is not a traditional novel with a clearly defined plot and carefully orchestrated resolution of one or more central problems. It has been variously described as a "compendium of contemporary uncertainty,"[1] "a grand satire of the dying Austria,"[2] and "the supreme example in Western literature of the novel of ideas."[3] The author himself characterized it as a novel "of a spiritual adventure," and as a "combat document." More than anything else, however, it is his strongest illustration of the creative power of his own sense of possibility.

The uniqueness of *The Man without Qualities* lies in the

fact that on one level it is an analysis of historical reality, while on another it is an extremely complex metaphor for something that transcends the limits of specifically defined time and locale.

With reference to the real world, Musil was concerned about the human developments in Austrian society that inevitably led in the direction of World War I. In his notes about the novel's orientation and his approach to the material, he defines its artistic focus by saying that direct portrayal of the period leading up to the war must be the real substance of the narration, the context to which the plot can be tied, and the thought that provides the orientation for everything else.

It is important to understand that what mattered most for Musil were questions of human response to a spiritual atmosphere, and not the details of events. In his interview with Oskar Maurus Fontana in 1926, he disclaimed engagement in the writing of a historical novel, insisting that the actual explanation of concrete events did not interest him. One reason for this posture was that he considered facts to be totally interchangeable. Accordingly, he declared his fascination with what is spiritually typical, "the phantom aspect of the happening."[4] For Musil, that "phantom aspect" is a timeless dimension of human experience. In the impact of events upon the individual, it is the factor that stimulates experimentation with new ideas.

Within the framework of *The Man without Qualities*, Musil treats what he sees as major problems of the immediate prewar years—the search for order and conviction, the role of the "Other Condition" in the life of the individual, the situation of the scientific person—as substance for experiments with ideas about achieving utopian forms of existence. His notes to the novel identify the most important of the projected patterns as three separate utopias. The first of these is the utopia of the given social condition, the second, the utopia of the "Other Condition" as found in love, and the third, a purely refined form of the "Other Condition" with mystical implications. In discussing these possibilities, he suggests that they differ in importance and that they can be reduced to two major utopias, that of real life and that of the "Millennial Kingdom," where the latter is a combination of the respective forms of the "Other Condition" experienced through love and mysticism.

The experiments pertaining to the first alternative receive their greatest emphasis in the early portions of the book. Exploration of the potentialities of the "Other Condition" then follows as the development of ideas for their own sake reaches its strongest intensity. Because Musil believed that attainment of the "Other Condition" could never be permanent in rational mortality, he projected an ending for the novel that would lead the central characters back into reality.

Musil's experiments with the search for utopia take the form of exposing his "guinea pig" to various stimuli and observing the results. The "guinea pig" is Ulrich, a representative specimen of technological man who is characterized by himself and others as a "man without qualities." The stimuli to which he responds include people who stand for different aspects of modern society, social, political, cultural, and intellectual situations that are typical of the times, and ideas that represent possibilities for alternate approaches to life and its questions. In each instance, the object of the experiment is to obtain a solution to a single puzzle. As the novel's male protagonist sums it up for his sister, the problem that troubles him most is concentrated in the question: "How am I to live?"

The outcome of each investigation is at once a function of and a contribution to the view of typical modern scientific man as a "man without qualities." On one level at least, the entire novel revolves around what it means to be such an individual. For Musil, a "man without qualities" is today's manifestation of the man of possibility, unfixed man in all his ambivalence and ambiguity. In defining the title figure as a typical representative of the times, one of his friends describes him as a man who always knows what to do, a man who can look into a woman's eyes, a man who is intelligent and able to use his mental capacities well under all conditions. More striking are the polarities that exist within him. In addition to talents of strength, objectivity, courage, and endurance, he can be either impetuous or cool and cautious. He can laugh when he is angry, reject things that stir his soul, and find good in things that are bad. His relationship to the world is completely unstable, because his surroundings represent infinite changing possibilities.

It is precisely this fluidity of his nature and his lack of a strong sense of reality, however, that make the "man without qualities" the ideal vehicle for Musil's experiments. His sense of possibility is manifested in a conscious utopianism that is a direct product of his intellectual mobility. It permits him to treat life as a laboratory and to contemplate the uniting of opposites to achieve a more fulfilling existence.

Ulrich's attempts to redefine his life are projected against a rich and complex fabric of interpersonal, social, political, and psychological relationships. At the age of thirty-two, he has behind him three unsuccessful endeavors to become a "man of importance," first as an officer, then as an engineer, and finally as a mathematician. These efforts have been in vain because he is more at home in the realm of possibility than in the mundane real world. Accordingly, in response to what he perceives as a lack of order and meaning in his existence as a whole, he decides to take a year's vacation from his normal life. During that period, he hopes to discover the causes of his surrounding reality's progressive collapse and a more suitable direction for his own future. The body of the novel is formed by the composite presentation of what he learns about himself and his environment in the course of this experiment.

To the extent that one can trace even a general story line for the completed portion of the fragment, its substance can be divided into two major sections with numerous subgroupings of connected situations, ideas, events, observations, and characters. The first main portion examines approximately half of the "vacation" year. It is primarily a description of Ulrich's efforts and ultimate failure to find an appropriate niche for himself within the context of Austrian prewar reality.

Diverse aspects of the decaying society are illuminated in a panorama of character types and behavioral patterns, as Musil depicts Ulrich's involvement in an empty political project called "the Collateral Campaign." Ulrich's participation consists primarily of passive observation of and reflection about events and situations. This fact determines the form of the narration. Essayistic integration of ideas, rather than elaboration of action and plot, receives the key emphasis.

In the second half of the narrative, the Collateral Campaign moves into the background as Ulrich abandons his attempt to find the right life for himself within the domain of material reality. His search enters a new phase in the intense exploration of the possibilities for fulfillment offered by the "Other Condition." The problem of finding the proper form of existence becomes that of self-definition as he grapples with the question of his relationship to his sister Agathe.

With this narrowing of focus comes a subtle change in the format of artistic presentation. Ulrich's examinations of a broad spectrum of ideas about love and mysticism are elaborated in long conversations between brother and sister. In the process of these discussions the siblings begin to function as complementary halves of a single spiritual unit.

How the author intended to end the novel is the subject of continuing controversy among Musil scholars. It is clear from unfinished fragments of chapters, notes from different periods of work on the novel, statements in interviews, and comments in letters that he considered many variations and possibilities for concluding his masterpiece. Nevertheless, only two things can be determined with relative certainty: First, Ulrich's experiments with both mysticism and love would fail to yield a final satisfying answer, just as the attempts to adapt to practical reality had done. Second, his "vacation" year would end with the protagonists and their world being swallowed up by the war. In the notes to the novel; where he projects the ultimate collapse of the Agathe-Ulrich relationship, Musil characterizes the combination of Ulrich's decision to participate in the war and the miscarriage of their excursion into the "Other Condition" as the "end of the utopias."

One of the most significant features of *The Man without Qualities* is Musil's general portrayal of prewar Austria as the setting for his "adventure of the spirit." Kakania, as he calls the dying Austro-Hungarian monarchy, is a land for which spiritual inertia is characteristic. In retrospect, he describes the vanished Austria of former years as an unacknowledged model for many things, a place where speed existed, but not very much of it. Despite the genius that it has produced in the past, it has lost its cultural energy: "It was the State that was by now only just, as it were, acquiescing in its own existence." For that reason, it is ripe for some historical event that will bring about radical changes and move things in a new direction.

A major part of Musil's purpose in writing his critical analysis of the times was to demonstrate how such conditions must inevitably lead to the explosive consequences of war. In that respect, the invented characters and situations of the narrative become symbols and metaphors for broad social and political phenomena.

Despite its de-emphasis in the later portions of the novel, the Collateral Campaign provides what Werner Welzig has labeled "the thread of action that holds the work together."[5] On the surface, the project is simply an endeavor to give Austria new visibility in the world, through the creation in 1918 of a yearlong seventieth anniversary celebration of the reign of Emperor Franz Josef. It is conceived as a direct response to the planned Prussian commemoration of Wilhelm II's thirty years on the throne, an event scheduled for the same year. Within the narrative framework, committee meetings and planning sessions, individual responses to the envisioned festivities, and discussions of the action's implications are employed as vehicles for the presentation of a wide variety of representative Austrian social types. The Collateral Campaign thus becomes on a deeper level Musil's focal metaphor for the spirit of the era. That point is hammered home in the author's notes to the final portion of the work, where he says that the Collateral Campaign will lead to the war.

Musil's ironic treatment of the prevailing social, cultural, and political attitudes in prewar Vienna is extremely successful from an artistic point of view. In the diverse reactions to the Collateral Campaign he offers a stark picture of the pathological condition of an Austrian society made up of people great and small, all of whom are concerned only with their own trivial or glorious schemes while the empire staggers on the edge of collapse.

The portrayed perceptions of the grand patriotic endeavor are as disparate as the characters and the parts of the national community that they represent. Count Leinsdorf, for example, views the coming celebration as an opportunity for Austria to reclaim its true essence. Ulrich's friend Clarisse becomes obsessed with the idea of promoting an Austrian Nietzsche Year. Associated with that, she wants to do something for the homicidal maniac Moosbrugger. For still another figure, the appropriate action is the establishment of an Emperor Franz Josef Anniversary Soup Kitchen.

At the same time, broad factions within the society greet the whole idea with skepticism and suspicion. Already-existing tensions are intensified when ethnic minorities come to regard the project as a Pan-Germanic plot, while extremists in the other direction view it as threatening to destroy the German nation both spiritually and intellectually.

Marie-Louise Roth has summarized effectively the function of the proposed patriotic demonstration in exposing the society's mortal weaknesses. She says:

The Collateral Campaign that was invented by Musil illustrates in its main representatives the false values of an era, the abstract idealism, the confusion of the spirit, the bureaucratism, the phraseology, the impersonalism, the nonsense and the sterility of all endeavors. . . . The leading persons of the Collateral Campaign live and act according to fossilized principles, the unsuitability and falseness of which they feel themselves.[6]

Ulrich's response to the Collateral Campaign is especially important because it illuminates the project as a parody of his own individual quest for life's meaning. As the figures who promote the cause of celebrating the prolonged reign of their "Emperor of Peace" continue to search for a powerful focus for the undertaking, Ulrich makes his own suggestion as to what the movement should accomplish. Speaking to Count Leinsdorf, he proposes that the Collateral Campaign initiate a general spiritual inventory, as though Judgment Day were coming in 1918, signaling the end of the old spiritual era and the dawning of a higher one. He concludes his presentation by stating that until an official institution is created that is responsible for precision and the spirit, other goals remain either unattainable or illusory.

It is significant that nobody takes Ulrich's recommendation seriously, not even Ulrich himself. Just as the very nature of the spirit of the times will not permit a true synthesis of reality and the soul on a national scale, so Ulrich's own goal for himself cannot be realized because his attitude of "active passivism" (Musil's term for passivity masked by meaningless action) prevents a similar synthesis on an individual plane.

There is stark irony in the parallel between the results of Ulrich's "active passivism" approach to his search for the right life and the accomplishments of the Collateral Campaign in its attempt to renew Austria's sense of identity. At one point the protagonist clarifies his stance with respect to external events by comparing it to that of a prisoner who is waiting for the opportunity to escape. While emphasizing the anticipation of action, the image conveys the tension that exists in a situation of static longing for something that never materializes. Pursued to one possible conclusion, it suggests that escape from confinement may occur only as the prisoner experiences his own execution.

Similarly, the progress of the Collateral Campaign is limited to the maintaining of expectation concerning potential future activity. The pattern of "active passivism" is underscored most strongly in what one character calls "the slogan of action." When it becomes apparent that the semiofficial planning committee is accomplishing nothing, Count Leinsdorf utters a hollow watchcry for its continued wheel spinning. He says that something has to be done. Because the Collateral Campaign, like its secretary Ulrich, is representative of the zeitgeist, its response to Leinsdorf's challenge is the same as his. Nothing happens beyond the contemplation of possibilities.

To the extent that the movement's failure to act symbolizes Austria's passivity toward the conditions leading to the war, the outcome is the same as for Ulrich's prisoner. Release from the waiting comes about only through the empire's destruction. As Wilfried Berghahn has pointed out, that fact becomes apparent at the moment when Ulrich first learns of the Collateral Campaign's existence through his father's letter: "For the father's letter, of course, acquires the satirical function that is decisive for the novel only through the dating of the Austrian apotheosis in the death year of the monarchy. With that, the Collateral Campaign is characterized from the first moment on as a burial undertaking. Its protagonists become the masters of ceremonies for a modern *danse macabre*. They just do not know it yet."[7]

The project's function as a metaphor for the disintegration of a stagnant order is further emphasized in the lifelessness of the interpersonal relationships experienced by its actual and would-be participants. As Ulrich makes his way back and forth among the "death-dancers," observing and experimenting with them, his encounters reveal both the tenuousness and fragility of existing connections and an increasing inability to establish new, meaningful bonds based on traditional concepts of love and affinity. This accentuation of isolation and alienation is visible not only in the way in which other figures respond to Ulrich, but also in the manner of their interaction among themselves.

A vivid illustration of the Collateral Campaign's lack of power to bring about unifying change is given in the figure of Ulrich's cousin Diotima Tuzzi, whose drawing room is the planning committee's headquarters. In the picture of Viennese society that Musil creates, Diotima is the bourgeois defender of a romantic vision of Austrian culture. She views the Collateral Campaign as a unique opportunity to realize on a practical level the things that are of greatest importance. For her, the paramount goal is the rediscovery of "that 'human unity' in man's life which has been lost because of the advent of modern materialism and scientific reasoning."[8] Yet her inability to achieve anything more than superficial oneness with others is demonstrated clearly in her respective relationships with her husband, Ulrich, and the Prussian Arnheim.

The impractical, idealistic notions that Diotima cultivates in her salon only estrange her from her bureaucrat spouse. Tuzzi, whom Ulrich sees as the embodiment of pure, practical manliness, is totally absorbed in his profession. He feels no kinship at all with those involved in extracurricular intellectual pursuits. Accordingly, in the scenes where he appears, he is an outsider looking in at the peculiar world of Diotima's involvement in the Collateral Campaign.

Diotima is unable to realize any sort of deep personal union with Ulrich for at least two reasons. On a purely matter-of-fact level, the two cousins possess sharply different attitudes and personalities. That is, Ulrich is the embodiment of Musil's idea of healthy, scientific man, while Diotima represents what is unrealistic and decadent in the contemporary world. More important is the fact that for Ulrich, Diotima is simply another subject for detached experimental observation. Ulrich is prepared to enter only an intellectual relationship governed by carefully controlled conditions. He suggests that they try to love each other like fictional characters who meet in a work of literature, leaving out the superficial padding that gives reality a phony appearance of fatness. Because Diotima's spiritual focus is at best counterfeit intellectual, she is incapable of playing the role that Ulrich envisions for her, and the experiment fails before it begins.

In its meaning for the novel as a whole, the most important of Diotima's vain attempts to unite with another individual is her abortive liaison with Arnheim. A Prussian industrialist and writer whom Musil modeled after Walther Rathenau, Arnheim plays the role of Ulrich's spiritual antagonist. His hollow affair with Diotima thus becomes a shadowy parody of the intense Ulrich-Agathe involvement that dominates the second half of *The Man without Qualities*.

During the course of her participation in the Collateral Campaign, Arnheim becomes a peculiar symbol for the irrationality of Diotima's perception of the project. Under the spell of his external facade, she comes to view him as a kindred spirit with whom she can bring to pass the cultural rejuvenation that she sees as the campaign's goal. Her quixotic approach to her self-made task is given its most grotesque manifestation in her grand idea that her Prussian friend must become the spiritual leader of the Collateral Campaign, despite the fact that it competes jealously with a concurrent celebration in Prussia-Germany.

On the surface, Arnheim appears to share Diotima's vision of their common cause, and he does little to discourage her growing attachment to him. As their spiritual relationship grows stronger, the Collateral Campaign becomes for the two of them an island of refuge. It takes on the dimensions of a special destiny that shapes their lives at a critical moment. As they participate in the project, they grow to share the perception that it represents an enormous intellectual opportunity and responsibility. For that reason, Diotima eventually reaches the point where she considers leaving her husband and marrying Arnheim in order to make their apparent spiritual union permanent. That plan collapses under the strain of reality's intrusion into her romantic illusion. The process of events uncovers the fact that Arnheim's real interest in her salon has little or nothing to do with the Collateral Campaign. He has simply exploited the situation to make business contacts. The envisioned union of souls founders on his pragmatism.

In its artistic function as a recurring symbol for Musil's main ideas, the Collateral Campaign spins within the novel a structural thread that binds together key character groups and situations. Parallel to it, although receiving less emphasis, is a second strand of thought that fulfills a similar purpose, reinforcing the author's statements about the prewar Austrian world by illuminating it from an entirely different direction. The resulting contribution to the narrative fabric is one of harsh, chaotic color in sharp contrast to the more subdued, passive hues of the Collateral Campaign's characteristic inaction.

At the center of this more threatening representation of the spirit of the times is a symbol for what one critic has called "the insanity of a world out of control."[9] It takes the form of the homicidal maniac Christian Moosbrugger.

Like the Collateral Campaign, Moosbrugger provides stimuli to which the various figures respond, revealing things about themselves and the society of which they are a part. Through the brutal slaying and mutilation of his prostitute victims, he arouses peculiar feelings within others, feelings that throw into question traditional concepts of social normality. The judicial system's visible inability to ascertain his mental competence and his accountability for his actions becomes a grotesque caricature of what is happening on the other levels of the novel. His apparent rationality in the courtroom parallels the facade of reason that conceals the tragic internal decay of the social order. According to Musil, Moosbrugger reflects the pertinent conditions within the surrounding environment, as if they were seen in a broken mirror.

Ulrich's views concerning him are especially important for the elucidation of Moosbrugger's meaning for the work. For Ulrich, Moosbrugger is the inevitable product of the world's collective irrationality. In one instance, the thought occurs to him that if it were possible for mankind to dream in unison, the resulting vision would be Moosbrugger.

Because the murderer's behavior is not bound by the restrictions of reason, he is able to participate in the life of a realm beyond material reality, where the "goodness" of an action is determined entirely by individual perception. In that respect, he becomes a perverse manifestation of transcendence into the "Other Condition," where the sense of possibility is unfettered by a traditional morality based upon external social standards. As Johannes Loebenstein has observed: "In this murderer . . . Ulrich sees all of humanity's possibilities combined together in a radically paradoxical unity."[10]

Just as Arnheim functions as Ulrich's antagonist in the practical, material world, so Moosbrugger plays the role of his opposite in the domain of the spirit. A significant aspect of Ulrich's search for fulfillment is his attempt to establish his complete identity by finding and uniting with the missing feminine component of his soul. His experiments with a number of different women bring him no closer to that ideal until he finally rediscovers his spiritual "Siamese twin," in his sister Agathe. In the figure of Moosbrugger, on the other hand, the image of a society that rejects and destroys spiritual completeness is given its strongest elaboration. What the murderer achieves in killing his victims is the excision of the unwanted feminine dimension from his own being. That fact is made abundantly clear in the narrator's description of one of the murders.

In the scene in question, Moosbrugger is presented lying rolled up in a ticket booth, with his head in the corner, pretending to be asleep. Next to him lies a prostitute who has attached herself to him during the night. The narrator labels her Moosbrugger's "accursed second self." When the psychopath tries to slip away from her in the dark, she holds him back, wrapping her arms around his neck. His response is to pull out his knife and stab her with it. When she falls with her head inside the booth, he drags her out, stabbing her repeatedly until he is satisfied that he has "cut her completely away from himself."

The behavior of Moosbrugger's victim is especially meaningful for the scene that is presented here. It signals that within the destructively insane world symbolized by the murderer the feminine element seeks undeterably for the union that he rejects. That idea is given even greater emphasis in the descriptions of Ulrich's interactions with Clarisse, Moosbrugger's strongest female spiritual counterpart.

During the course of the novel, Clarisse becomes progressively more obsessed with the idea of a personal mission to transform European society. Within the context of that fixation, she comes to view herself as a "double being." Intrigued by her husband Walter's fear that she is going insane, she associates the awareness of man's inherent doubleness with that insanity, and she concludes that modern "normal" society has lost its knowledge of humanity's true nature. Pointing to what she sees as a precedent in classical antiquity, she talks about representations of Apollo as both man and woman, insisting that human beings, like the Greek gods, are dual in nature. When Walter presses her to define her own duality more specifically, she responds that she is both man and woman. From this time on, she identifies more and more strongly with the concept of the hermaphrodite.

Clarisse's conscious association of insanity with the redemptive power of the dual individual draws her to Moosbrugger. She begins a crusade to set him free. Within her thoughts he becomes a particularly potent example of the double man. Specifically, she views him as the embodiment of her own mission to unite within herself the opposing extremes of the male element, identified in her mind with the figures of Christ and Nietzsche respectively. For that reason, she tries to persuade Ulrich to help her break Moosbrugger out of prison. She believes that if he can be freed, the redemption of the society will be the result.

To a large extent, Clarisse and Moosbrugger are symbols for

what Musil saw as the ultimate focal idea of the novel, carried to its pathological extreme. The starkness of their portrayal sets off through contrast a more contemplative, philosophical development of the author's concept of human duality. The latter is presented during the progress of what the narrator describes as "a journey to the furthest limits of the possible, skirting the dangers of the impossible and unnatural, even of the repulsive, and perhaps not always quite avoiding them." This "journey" is Ulrich's final attempt to find the missing portion of his own identity. It takes place as he seeks to enter the "Other Condition" through the increasingly intense relationship with his sister.

In an important passage from his notebook, Musil suggests that the nucleus for *The Man without Qualities* is contained in an early poem that he wrote, entitled "Isis und Osiris" (Isis and Osiris). Both for its relevance to the discussion of the Ulrich-Agathe portion of the novel, and as one of few surviving examples of Musil's early awkward experimentation with lyric forms, the poem is presented here in its entirety:

Isis and Osiris

On the leaves of the stars the moon-boy lay
Sleeping silvery dim,
And the sun-wheel on its way
Turned around and gazed at him.
From the desert came the red wind's wail,
And along the coast there is no sail.

And his sister softly from the sleeper
Cut his manhood free, did it consume.
And she gave her soft red heart then for it,
Placed it on him in his organ's room.
And in dream the wound again grew whole.
And she ate the lovely sex she stole.

Lo, then roared aloud the sunlight,
As the sleeper started from his sleep,

Stars were tossing, just as rowboats
Moored on chains will surge and dart
When the mighty tempests start.

Lo, his brothers, rage asmoulder,
Chased the robber winsome, fair,
And he then his bow did shoulder,
And the blue space broke in there,
Woods collapsed beneath their tread,
And the stars ran with them filled with dread.
    Yet none caught the slim, bird-shouldered maiden,
    Not a one, despite how far he ran.

He alone, the young boy whom she called at night,
Finds her when the moon and sun are changing,
Of all hundred brothers none but this,
And he eats her heart, and she eats his.

There is a direct textual link between *The Man without Qualities* and the myth presented in the poem. In a conversation with his newly rediscovered sister, Ulrich attempts to describe the startlingly intense attraction that exists between them. In doing so, he refers to a variety of myths, including that of the human being divided into two, Pygmalion, Hermaphroditus, and the legend of Isis and Osiris. He points to these models as examples of a historic human craving for a double of the opposite sex.

The basis for the connection between the poem and the second half of the novel lies in Musil's interest in the Egyptian sun god Osiris and his sister-wife, the moon goddess Isis, as archetypal symbols for the love between brother and sister. The author was fascinated by these particular figures because Isis represents the irrational, metaphysical dimension, while her brother is identified with the opposing material and rational elements. Unification of these separate halves, graphically signified in the poem by the exchange of hearts and in the novel by Agathe's longing to trade bodies with Ulrich, connotes the merging of fundamental antithetical tendencies of mortality through the power of love.

As ultimately developed within the novel, the longing for completion of the self, which is the focus of "Isis and Osiris," is Musil's most extreme projection of the sense of possibility. It is the motivation for Ulrich's attempt to join Agathe in the Utopia of the "Other Condition" through actualization of what Marie-Louise Roth has called "the felt inkling of unity between spirit and nature, subject and object, the dream of termination of the duality between 'I' and 'you.' "[11]

Ulrich's first meeting with his sister after their father's death sets the tone for the intimate union that develops between them. The two siblings encounter each other similarly clothed, so that Agathe immediately characterizes them as "twins." As Ulrich forms his initial impression of her, an idea surfaces that is explored in ever-intensifying variation through the remainder of the novel. While considering her attributes, he notes that she is neither patently emancipated nor bohemian, in spite of the peculiar clothing in which she has received him. The more he attempts to penetrate to the essence of her nature, the more he is struck with the idea that there is something hermaphrodite about her.

In the descriptions of subsequent encounters, ever-more emphasis is placed upon the notion that Agathe is Ulrich's female alter ego. One scene presents him as seeing himself approaching in the figure of Agathe as she enters a room. To be sure, this other person is more beautiful than he is, and she has an aura about her that he does not see in himself, but he cannot help but think that she is really himself, repeated and somehow changed. It is this feeling that she embodies the longed for missing aspect of his identity that moves Ulrich to suggest to her the experiment of living together in a new kind of union beyond the restraints of conventional social reality. His vision of their spiritual merging in the ideal realm that he calls "the Millenium, the Kingdom of a Thousand Years" suggests the attainment of fulfillment in absolute interdependence, not only with each other, but also with the world as a whole.

The process of unification is one of withdrawal from the

concerns of material reality into a condition of shared contemplation. Together, Ulrich and Agathe explore many ideas about man's physical and spiritual nature, his actual and possible situation in the world, and the means by which the individual may transcend the traditional limits of mortal existence. Dense conversations about love, mysticism, and morality are part of the "search for a state in which the individual is enhanced, in which his ego rises and does not fall."[12]

In the Agathe-Ulrich dialogues Musil presents the elements of his theory of a psychology of feeling, the bases of which are his interpretations of Nietzsche's ideas concerning private and general morality, the era of comparison, the logic of dreams, suffering and compassion, love and justice. In many instances, complete chapters are devoted to essayistic elaboration of theoretical points and abstractions, interrupting the flow of the narrative with material that Musil eventually recognized as being out of place in the novel. Even for the careful reader, these passages form an unnecessary barrier to the clear understanding of the author's artistic objectives.

Through the exchange of ideas, Ulrich and Agathe draw nearer to each other, until they begin to think in concert. As their relationship approaches the peak of its intensity, the narrator describes them as feeling as if they were a single entity, working together in a harmony similar to that of people who play the piano four-handed, or people who read the same material together aloud. On a mystical, dreamlike level, they seem to melt together and become one being, sharing a common personality.

The peculiar ambiguity of their situation at this point is underscored in the designation that they give to themselves: "the unseparated and not united ones." It suggests that their union, despite its spiritual depth, is fragile and unstable. Recognition that the bond between them may collapse causes them first to contemplate suicide, then to continue the experiment to its final extreme. Agathe gives the signal for the beginning of its last stage when she says that they will not kill themselves until they have exhausted every other possibility for resolving their situation.

The climactic event of the novel is a combination of physical and spiritual union, in which incest serves as a catalyst for the final shattering of all boundaries between brother and sister. In one of the novel fragments, Musil describes them as coming together physically like animals seeking warmth. In the process of sexual union, a spiritual merging occurs on another level, and each of them has the feeling of having assimilated the other. Time and space lose their meaning as the lovers transcend all previous experience and enter the absolute realm of the "Other Condition."

Although the protagonists of *The Man without Qualities* do achieve self-completion temporarily, it is clear that Musil did not envision them finding a permanent escape from conventional reality in their mystical utopia. As he expressed it to Oskar Maurus Fontana during their celebrated interview, the attempt to prolong the experience fails because the absolute state cannot be maintained.[13] In that assessment, as in the novel itself, he gave a lasting indictment of a world progressing toward war, in which only a "man without qualities" could survive.

8

Life Is an Idea

"What matters to me is the passionate energy of the thought. Where I cannot elaborate some special idea, the work immediately becomes too boring for me; that is true for almost every single paragraph." In these words, entered in his journal in 1910, Musil captured the essence of an approach to the creation of literature that would continue to shape his art throughout the rest of his career. Ideas for their own sake became the focus of his writings because his perception of belles lettres demanded that what he wrote present something new, something that could add to man's spiritual and intellectual wealth.

From Musil's perspective, events, characters, situations, and places are not new, but rather completely interchangeable. For that reason, within his literary works they remain at best secondary in importance, symbols for something deeper, overshadowed by the manifestations of man's inner life that form the only true source of what is unique and different.

Most of the ideas explored by Musil in his novels, stories, dramas, and essays relate to the interpretation rather than the description of two kinds of human experience. The tension between rational encounters with fixed reality and experiences within the subjective, changing, infinite domain of feeling provides the impetus for his intensely personal treatments of contemporary problems.

Like other writers of his time, Musil was deeply concerned with aspects of the modern mortal condition that foster alienation, isolation, and introversion. The theme of individual loneliness is a constant feature of his writings that recurs in seemingly endless variation. His protagonists, beginning with Törless, and including Thomas, Regine, Veronika, Claudine, Homo, Ketten, Tonka, Ulrich, and Agathe, are lonely, introverted people who seek for meaning, identity, and completeness in their lives, and fail to find what they are looking for within the restrictive limits of conventional reality. What makes these figures different from those portrayed by other authors, however, is the emphasis that Musil places upon a sense of possibility that enables them to look beyond the physical, material here and now, and to transcend, however briefly, the traditional barriers to *new* experience.

Musil's dissatisfaction with the constraints of established systems, whether social or political, ethical or artistic, contributes to his works a quality of endless openness. They give no clearcut, definitive answers to the questions that are raised, no final resolution of tensions and conflicts, no basis in absolutes for progress toward answers or resolution. By leaving the reader ever hovering between subjective and objective reality, between fantasy and fact, between rational thought and feeling, between concrete substance and metaphor, the author forces his audience to come to grips with life as a domain in which a measure of fulfillment can be achieved only in the ceaseless exploration of infinite possibilities contained in human ideas. To that extent at least, his writings achieve the purpose that he defined for them in the essay "Über Robert Musils Bücher" (On Robert Musil's books). There he took the position that creative writing is the portrayal of life, after the writer has thought about it, and that understanding the human content of a literary work requires the ability to plot an infinite chain of thought and feeling that reflects things as diverse as diction, the figures themselves, and the subtleties that cannot be reproduced concretely.

During his lifetime and in the years following his death, most of the writings of Robert Musil held appeal only for a relatively limited readership. Even today they remain largely unattractive to a broad public, because they demand of their audience what their author demanded of himself as an artist: an unwavering commitment to the idea as an absolute value, a willingness, even an eagerness to explore possibilities that go beyond normally accepted limits and standards, and a restless dissatisfaction with things that refuse to admit the potential for change.

Notes

1. A Dissatisfied Life

1. Robert Musil, *Tagebücher* (Reinbek bei Hamburg: Rowohlt, 1976), vol. 1, 936. All subsequent quotations from the diaries are taken from this edition. Quotations from Musil's letters come from the two-volume edition *Briefe 1901–1942* (Reinbek bei Hamburg: Rowohlt, 1980). The texts quoted from his essays are found in the second volume of the newer Frisé edition of the collected works, *Prosa und Stücke, Kleine Prosa, Aphorismen, Autobiographisches, Essays und Reden* (Reinbek bei Hamburg: Rowohlt, 1978), and the material from *Vinzenz and the Girl Friend of Important Men* comes from the same volume. Translations from the German of these, the poem "Isis and Osiris," and all secondary sources are mine. Texts quoted from the novels and novellas are found in the translations by Eithne Wilkins and Ernst Kaiser, specifically: *Young Törless* (New York: Pantheon, 1955), *The Man without Qualities*, 3 vols, (London: Secker and Warburg, 1953–1960), and *Five Women* (New York: Delacorte Press, 1966). A few translations from *The Man without Qualities* are mine. They come from the first volume of the 1978 edition of the collected works and are renderings of passages not included in the Wilkins-Kaiser volumes. Andrea Simon's translation of *The Enthusiasts* (New York: Performing Arts Journal Publications, 1983) is the source for material from that play.

2. Hugo von Hofmannsthal, "Der Dichter und diese Zeit," in *Gesammelte Werke in Einzelausgaben: Prosa II* (Frankfurt am Main: Fischer, 1951), pp. 280–281.

3. Wilfried Berghahn, *Robert Musil* (Reinbeck bei Hamburg: Rowohlt, 1963), p. 25.

4. For a discussion of this relationship see Elisabeth Albertsen, "Ju-

135

gendsünden?," in *Robert Musil: Studien zu seinem Werk*, eds. Karl Dinklage, Elisabeth Albertsen, and Karl Corino (Reinbek bei Hamburg: Rowohlt, 1970), p. 20.

5. Karl Dinklage, "Musils Herkunft und Lebensgeschichte," in *Robert Musil: Leben, Werk, Wirkung*, ed. Karl Dinklage (Reinbek bei Hamburg: Rowohlt, 1960), p. 219.
6. Musil, *Briefe 1901–1942*, vol 1, p. 143.
7. Ibid., p. 182.
8. Quoted in Helmut Gumtau, *Robert Musil* (Berlin: Colloquium, 1967), p. 33.
9. Quoted in Karl Baedeker, "Robert Musil und ein junger Mann seiner Zeit," in *Robert Musil: Studien zu seinem Werk*, p. 335.
10. Musil, *Briefe 1901–1942*, vol 1, p. 1439.

2. The Other Condition: *Young Törless*

1. Harry Goldgar, "The Square Root of Minus One: Freud and Robert Musil's 'Törless,' " *Comparative Literature* 17 (1965), p. 118.
2. For his discussion of this point see the essay "Über Robert Musils Bücher" in *Prosa und Stücke, Kleine Prosa, Aphorismen, Autobiographisches, Essays und Reden*, p. 997.
3. Ibid.
4. Siegfried Rönisch, "Robert Musil: Ein Versuch über sein Leben und Werk," *Weimarer Beiträge* 30 (1984), p. 933.
5. Uwe Baur, "Zeit- und Gesellschaftskritik in Robert Musils Roman 'Die Verwirrungen des Zöglings Törleß,' " in *Vom Törleß zum Mann ohne Eigenschaften*, eds. Uwe Baur and Dietmar Goltschnigg (Munich and Salzburg: Fink, 1973), p. 32.
6. Frederick G. Peters, *Robert Musil, Master of the Hovering Life* (New York: Columbia University Press, 1978), p. 42.
7. Yvon Desportes, "Vergleichende Untersuchung eines Stils und einer Philosophie: Ein Werk Musils aus der Sicht Machs," in *Robert Musil*, ed. Renate von Heydebrand (Darmstadt: Wissenschaftliche Buchgesellschaft, 1982), p. 288.
8. Johannes Loebenstein, "Das Problem der Erkenntnis in Musils künstlerischem Werk," in *Robert Musil: Leben, Werk, Wirkung*, p. 87.

9. *Robert Musil*, p. 29.
10. Baur, "Zeit- und Gesellschaftskritik in Robert Musils Roman 'Die Verwirrungen des Zöglings Törleß,' " p. 36.
11. Various critics have interpreted this particular reflection as the beginning of Musil's preoccupation with the masculine-feminine split in the individual personality, a problem that is given its most intensive treatment in *The Man without Qualities*.

3. Looking Inside: *Unions*

1. Musil, "Über Robert Musils Bücher," 996.
2. Eithne Wilkins and Ernst Kaiser, "Musil und die Quadratwurzel aus minus Eins," in *Robert Musil: Leben, Werk, Wirkung*, p. 160.
3. Peters, *Robert Musil, Master of the Hovering Life*, p. 60.
4. Ibid., p. 65.
5. See for example Berghahn, *Robert Musil*, p. 60, and Osman Durrani, "*Die Vollendung der Liebe*: Apocalypse or Utopia?," in *Musil in Focus*, eds. Lothar Huber and John D. White (London: Institute of Germanic Studies, 1982), p. 16.
6. Peters, *Robert Musil, Master of the Hovering Life*, p. 69.
7. Rosemarie Zeller, " 'Die Versuchung der stillen Veronika'. Eine Untersuchung ihres Bedeutungsaufbaus," in *Sprachästhetische Sinnvermittlung*, eds. Dieter P. Farda and Ulrich Karthaus (Frankfurt am Main and Bern: Lang, 1982), pp. 135–36.
8. Peters, *Robert Musil, Master of the Hovering Life*, p. 74.
9. Ibid., p. 93.
10. Ibid., p. 89.

4. A Sense of Possibility: Two Dramas

1. Hellmuth Karasek, "Reisen in die verborgene Kindheit," *Der Spiegel* 39, no. 7 (11 February 1985), p. 199.
2. Sibylle Bauer, *Ethik und Bewußtheit*, in Sibylle Bauer and Ingrid Drevermann, *Studien zu Robert Musil* (Cologne and Graz: Böhlau, 1966), p. 7.

3. Günther Schneider, *Untersuchungen zum dramatischen Werk Robert Musils* (Bern and Frankfurt am Main: Lang, 1973), p. 147.

4. Ibid., p. 3.

5. Ibid., pp. 139–40.

6. Concerning the matter of what he expected of the actors, Musil wrote in his diary: "Most dramatists write in the manner that the actors speak; I demand that they speak the way I write."

7. Schneider, *Untersuchungen zum dramatischen Werk Robert Musils*, p. 54.

8. Bauer, *Ethik und Bewußtheit*, p. 8.

9. Ibid., p. 39.

10. Schneider, *Untersuchungen zum dramatischen Werk Robert Musils*, p. 62.

11. Ibid., p. 24.

12. Ibid., p. 26.

13. See especially Berghahn, *Robert Musil*, p. 85, and Schneider, *Untersuchungen zum dramatischen Werk Robert Musils*, p. 178.

14. Alfred Kerr, "Robert Musil: *Vinzenz und die Freundin bedeutender Männer*," *Berliner Tageblatt* 52, no. 560 (5 December 1923), as quoted in Karl Corino, "Robert Musil and Alfred Kerr," in *Robert Musil: Studien zu seinem Werk*, p. 264.

15. Schneider, *Untersuchungen zum dramatischen Werk Robert Musils*, p. 182.

16. Berghahn, *Robert Musil*, p. 86.

17. Egon Naganowski, " 'Vinzenz,' Oder der Sinn des sinnvollen Unsinns," in *Vom Törleß zum Mann ohne Eigenschaften*, eds. Uwe Baur and Dietmar Goltschnigg (Munich and Salzburg: Fink, 1973), p. 116.

18. Ibid., p. 119.

5. Man in Two Forms: *Three Women*

1. Letter to Musil from Norman Linker in Musil, *Briefe 1901–1942*, p. 460.

2. Peters, *Robert Musil, Master of the Hovering Life*, p. 116.

3. Ibid., p. 117.
4. Gumtau, *Robert Musil*, p. 36.
5. Peters, *Robert Musil, Master of the Hovering Life*, p. 106.
6. Gumtau, *Robert Musil*, p. 37.
7. Heinz-Peter Pütz, "Robert Musil," in *Deutsche Dichter der Moderne*, ed. Benno von Wiese (Berlin: Erich Schmidt, 1965), p. 311.
8. Loebenstein, "Das Problem der Erkenntnis in Musils künstlerischem Werk," in *Robert Musil: Leben, Werk, Wirkung*, p. 124.
9. See for example Peters, *Robert Musil, Master of the Hovering Life*, p. 106, and Gumtau, *Robert Musil*, p. 38.
10. Christine Oertel Sjögren, "Der Rätsel in Musils *Tonka*," in *Robert Musil*, p. 443.

6. In Quest of Another Kind of Human Being: The Essays

1. Musil, *Tagebücher*, vol 1, p. 643. Another title that he considered was *Detours*.
2. Gumtau, *Robert Musil*, p. 32.
3. Wilhelm Grenzmann, " 'Der Mann ohne Eigenschaften': Zur Problematik der Romangestalt," in *Robert Musil: Leben, Werk, Wirkung*, p. 57.
4. Gumtau, *Robert Musil*, p. 31.
5. Marie-Louise Roth, *Robert Musil: Ethik und Ästhetik* (Munich: List, 1972), p. 20.
6. Ibid., p. 32.
7. Susan Erickson, "Essay/Body/Fiction: The Repression of an Interpretive Context in an Essay of Robert Musil," *German Quarterly* 56/4 (1983), p. 582.
8. Oskar Maurus Fontana, "Erinnerungen an Robert Musil," in *Robert Musil: Leben, Werk, Wirkung*, p. 334.

7. Experimental Utopias: *The Man without Qualities*

1. Werner Welzig, *Der deutsche Roman im 20: Jahrhundert* (Stuttgart: Kröner, 1970), p. 9.

2. Wolfdietrich Rasch, "Robert Musil und sein Roman *Der Mann ohne Eigenschaften*," *Universitas* 9 (1954), p. 147.
3. Peters, *Robert Musil, Master of the Hovering Life*, p. 190.
4. Fontana, "Erinnerungen an Robert Musil," in *Robert Musil: Leben, Werk, Wirkung*, p. 338.
5. Welzig, *Der deutsche Roman im 20: Jahrhundert*, p. 192.
6. Marie-Louise Roth, "Robert Musil im Spiegel seines Werkes," in *Robert Musil: Leben, Werk, Wirkung*, p. 33.
7. Berghahn, *Robert Musil*, p. 95.
8. Peters, *Robert Musil, Master of the Hovering Life*, p. 205.
9. Gumtau, *Robert Musil*, p. 65.
10. Loebenstein, "Das Problem der Erkenntnis in Musils künstlerischem Werk," in *Robert Musil: Leben, Werk, Wirkung*, p. 94.
11. Roth, "Robert Musil im Spiegel seines Werkes," p. 21.
12. Wilhelm Braun, "Robert Musil," in *Encyclopedia of World Literature in the Twentieth Century* (New York: Ungar, 1983), vol 3, p. 337.
13. Fontana, "Erinnerungen an Robert Musil," p. 339.

Bibliography

I. Principal Books by Robert Musil in German

Die Verwirrungen des Zöglings Törleß. Leipzig: Wiener Verlag, 1906.
Beitrag zur Beurteilung der Lehren Machs. Berlin: Arnold, 1908.
Vereinigungen. Munich and Leipzig: Georg Müller, 1911.
Die Schwärmer. Dresden: Sibyllen-Verlag, 1921.
Grigia. Potsdam: Müller, 1923.
Die Portugiesin. Berlin: Rowohlt, 1923.
Drei Frauen. Berlin: Rowohlt, 1924.
Vinzenz und die Freundin bedeutender Männer. Berlin: Rowohlt, 1924.
Rede zur Rilke-Feier in Berlin am 16. 1. 1927. Berlin: Rowohlt, 1927.
Der Mann ohne Eigenschaften, 3 vols. Berlin: Rowohlt, 1930, 1933;
    Lausanne: Imprimierie centrale, 1943.
Nachlaß zu Lebzeiten. Zurich: Humanitas, 1936.
Über die Dummheit. Vienna: Bermann-Fischer, 1937.
Gesammelte Werke in Einzelausgaben, 3 vols. Hamburg: Rowohlt,
    1952–57.
Das hilflose Europa: Drei Essays. Munich: Piper, 1961.
Sämtliche Erzählungen. Reinbek bei Hamburg: Rowohlt, 1968.
Tagebücher, 2 vols. Reinbek bei Hamburg: Rowohlt, 1976.
Gesammelte Werke, 2 vols. Reinbek bei Hamburg: Rowohlt, 1978.
Briefe 1901–1942, 2 vols. Reinbek bei Hamburg: Rowohlt, 1980.

II. Works by Robert Musil in English Translation

The Man without Qualities, trans. Eithne Wilkins and Ernst Kaiser. 3
    vols. London: Secker and Warburg, 1953–60.
Young Törless, trans. Eithne Wilkins and Ernst Kaiser. London: Secker
    and Warburg, 1955; New York: Pantheon, 1955.

Tonka and Other Stories, trans. Eithne Wilkins and Ernst Kaiser. London: Secker and Warburg, 1965. American edition, *Five Women.* New York: Delacorte Press, 1966.

On Mach's Theories, trans. Kevin Mulligan. Washington, DC: Catholic University of America Press, 1982.

Pictures: An Excerpt from Posthumous While Still Alive, trans. Peter Wortsman. New York: Coalition of Publishers for Employment, 1983.

The Enthusiasts, trans. Andrea Simon. New York: Performing Arts Journal Publications, 1983.

III. Selected Books and Articles about Robert Musil

Albertsen, Elisabeth. *Ratio und "Mystik" im Werk Robert Musils.* Munich: Nymphenburger, 1968.

Althaus, Horst. *Zwischen Monarchie und Republik: Schnitzler, Hofmannsthal, Kafka, Musil.* Munich: Fink, 1976.

Appignanesi, Lisa. *Femininity and the Creative Imagination: A Study of Henry James, Robert Musil, and Marcel Proust.* New York: Barnes and Noble, 1973.

Arntzen, Helmut. *Musil-Kommentar.* Munich: Winkler, 1980.

Bauer, Sibylle, and Ingrid Drevermann. *Studien zu Robert Musil.* Cologne and Graz: Böhlau, 1966.

Baumann, Gerhart. *Robert Musil.* Bern and Munich: Francke, 1965.
———. "Robert Musil." *Handbook of Austrian Literature.* Edited by Frederick Ungar. New York: Ungar, 1973.

Baur, Uwe, and Elisabeth Castex, eds. *Robert Musil: Untersuchungen.* Königstein: Athenäum, 1980.

Baur, Uwe, and Dietmar Goltschnigg, eds. *Vom Törleß zum Mann ohne Eigenschaften.* Munich and Salzburg: Fink, 1973.

Beard, Philip H. "The 'End' of *The Man without Qualities.*" *Musil-Forum* 8 (1982): 30–45.

Berghahn, Wilfried. *Robert Musil.* Reinbek bei Hamburg: Rowohlt, 1963.

Braun, Wilhelm. "Robert Musil." *Encyclopedia of World Literature in the Twentieth Century,* 2d ed. Vol 3. New York: Ungar, 1983.

Brokoph-Mauch, Gudrun, ed. *Beiträge zur Musil-Kritik*. Bern and Frankfurt am Main: Lang, 1983.

Büren, Erhard von. *Zur Bedeutung der Psychologie im Werk Robert Musils*. Zurich: Atlantis, 1970.

Corino, Karl. *Robert Musils "Vereinigungen."* Munich: Fink, 1974.

Dinklage, Karl, ed. *Robert Musil: Leben, Werk, Wirkung*. Reinbek bei Hamburg: Rowohlt, 1960.

Dinklage, Karl, Elisabeth Albertsen, and Karl Corino, eds. *Robert Musil: Studien zu seinem Werk*. Reinbek bei Hamburg: Rowohlt, 1970.

Erickson, Susan. "Essay/Body/Fiction: The Repression of an Interpretive Context in an Essay of Robert Musil." *German Quarterly* 56 (1983): 580–93.

Farda, Dieter P., and Ulrich Karthaus, eds. *Sprachästhetische Sinnvermittlung*. Frankfurt am Main and Bern: Lang, 1982.

Freese, Wolfgang, ed. *Philologie und Kritik*. Munich and Salzburg: Fink, 1981.

Genno, Charles N. "Musil's Moral and Aesthetic Principles." *Orbis Literarum* 38 (1983): 140–49.

———. "Observations on Love and Death in Musil." *Neophilologus* 67 (1983): 118–25.

Gradischnig, Hertwig. *Das Bild des Dichters bei Robert Musil*. Munich: Fink, 1976.

Gumtau, Helmut. *Robert Musil*. Berlin: Colloquium, 1967.

Hagmann, Franz. *Aspekte der Wirklichkeit im Werke Robert Musils*. Bern: Lang, 1969.

Heyd, Dieter. *Musil-Lektüre, der Text, das Unbewußte*. Frankfurt am Main and Bern: Lang, 1980.

Heydebrand, Renate von, ed. *Robert Musil*. Darmstadt: Wissenschaftliche Buchgesellschaft, 1982.

Hickman, H. *Robert Musil and the Culture of Vienna*. La Salle, IL: Open Court, 1984.

Huber, Lothar, and John D. White, eds. *Musil in Focus*. London: Institute of Germanic Studies, 1982.

Jennings, Michael W. "Mystical Selfhood, Self-Delusion, Self-Dissolution: Ethical and Narrative Experimentation in Robert Musil's *Grigia*." *Modern Austrian Literature* 17/1 (1984): 59–77.

Kaiser, Ernst, and Eithne Wilkins. *Robert Musil. Eine Einführung in das Werk*. Stuttgart: Kohlhammer, 1962.

Kalow, Gert. *Zwischen Christentum und Ideologie*. Heidelberg: W. Rothe, 1956.

Karasek, Hellmuth. "Reisen in die verborgene Kindheit." *Der Spiegel* 39/7 (11 February 1985): 198–99.

Karthaus, Ulrich. *Der andere Zustand: Zeitstrukturen im Werke Robert Musils*. Berlin: E. Schmidt, 1965.

King, Lynda J. "The New Woman in Robert Musil's Comedy *Vinzenz und die Freundin bedeutender Männer*." *Modern Austrian Literature* 16/1 (1983): 23–36.

Krotz, Friedrich. *Interpretationen zu Robert Musil*. Munich: Oldenbourg, 1972.

Kühn, Dieter. *Analogie und Variation*. Bonn: Bouvier, 1965.

Luft, David S. *Robert Musil and the Crisis of European Culture*. Berkeley: University of California Press, 1980.

Mayer König, Wolfgang. *Robert Musils Möglichkeitsstil*. Vienna: Gesellschaft der Kunstfreunde, 1979.

Müller, Gerd. *Dichtung und Wissenschaft*. Stockholm: Almqvist and Wiksell, 1971.

Mulot, Sibylle. *Der junge Musil*. Stuttgart: Heinz, 1977.

Nusser, Peter. *Musils Romantheorie*. The Hague and Paris: Mouton, 1967.

Nutting, Peter West. "Uncaging Musil's *Amsel*." *Publications of the Modern Language Association* 98/1 (January 1983): 47–59.

Peters, Frederick G. *Robert Musil, Master of the Hovering Life*. New York: Columbia University Press, 1978.

Pike, Burton. *Robert Musil: An Introduction to His Work*. Ithica: Cornell University Press, 1961.

Pütz, Heinz-Peter. "Robert Musil." *Deutsche Dichter der Moderne*. Edited by Benno von Wiese. Berlin: E. Schmidt, 1965.

Rasch, Wolfdietrich. "Robert Musil und sein Roman *Der Mann ohne Eigenschaften*." *Universitas* 9 (1954): 145–51.

Reis, Gilbert. *Musils Frage nach der Wirklichkeit*. Königstein: Hain, 1983.

Rinderknecht, Siegfried. *Denkphantasie und Reflexionsleidenschaft*. Frankfurt am Main: R. G. Fischer, 1979.

Rönisch, Siegfried. "Robert Musil: Ein Versuch über sein Leben und Werk." *Weimarer Beiträge* 30/6 (1984): 926–53.

Roth, Marie-Louise, ed. *Bibliographie der zu Lebzeiten erschienenen*

Texte Robert Musils. Saarbrücken: Internationale Robert-Musil-Gesellschaft, 1984.

———. *Robert Musil: Ethik und Ästhetik.* Munich: List, 1972.

Röttger, Brigitte. *Erzählexperimente: Studien zu Robert Musils "Drei Frauen" und "Vereinigungen."* Bonn: Bouvier, 1973.

Schelling, Ulrich. *Identität und Wirklichkeit bei Robert Musil.* Zurich: Atlantis, 1968.

Schneider, Günther. *Untersuchungen zum dramatischen Werk Robert Musils.* Bern and Frankfurt am Main: Lang, 1973.

Strutz, Josef, and Johann Strutz, eds. *Robert Musil—Literatur, Philosophie, Psychologie.* Munich and Salzburg: Fink, 1984.

———. *Robert Musil und die kulturellen Tendenzen seiner Zeit.* Munich and Salzburg: Fink, 1983.

Thöming, Jürgen C. *Robert-Musil-Bibliographie.* Bad Homburg: Gehlen, 1968.

Welzig, Werner. *Der deutsche Roman im 20: Jahrhundert.* Stuttgart: Kröner, 1970.

Index